In God's Orchard

Cultivating the Fruit of a Spirit-Filled Life

NORTHWESTERN PUBLISHING HOUSE

Milwaukee, Wisconsin

Cover Illustrations: Lightstock
Designer: Lynda Williams

Northwestern Publishing House
N16W23379 Stone Ridge Drive, Waukesha WI 53188-1108
www.nph.net
© 2019 Northwestern Publishing House
Published 2019
Printed in the United States of America
ISBN 978-0-8100-3097-8
ISBN 978-0-8100-3098-5 (e-book)

21 22 23 24 25 26 27 28 29   10 9 8 7 6 5 4 3

Table
of
Contents

Introduction. v

Love . . . .*Amber Albee Swenson*. 1

Joy . . . . *Dr. Rhoda Wolle* 12

Peace . . . .*Amber Albee Swenson*. 24

Patience . . . . *Mollie Schairer*. 34

Kindness. . . . . *Mollie Schairer*. 43

Goodness . . . . . *Ann M. Ponath and Amber Albee Swenson* 53

Faithfulness . . . . *Naomi Schmidt* 63

Gentleness . . . .*Katie Martin*. 70

Self-Control . . . . *Naomi Schmidt* 80

Answers

Love 89

Joy 90

Peace 91

Patience 93

Kindness. 96

Goodness . . . . , , , , ... 99

Faithfulness 101

Gentleness 103

Self-Control 105

Introduction

In late July 2018, a three-person group formed with the sole task of helping Northwestern Publishing House put out the best women's Bible study possible. The three of us in the group (Naomi Schmidt, Mary Sieh, and I) are passionate, Bible-loving, women's Bible study teachers with many years of teaching among us.

Our goal was to create a Bible study that equips any woman anywhere to lead. While written for women by women, it would be reviewed and edited by a pastor, and answers would be provided. We wanted to take away the prep work and eliminate excuses to not be in the Word. Being in the Word with other women is hands down one of the dearest and richest blessings this side of heaven. It fortifies us to stand against Satan and everything the world and our sinful nature throws at us. And we want and need to stand, or we will certainly fall.

Early on we determined the first study should come not just from one voice but several voices. What a blessing it was that others with the same passion came alongside us and lent their voices to ours.

If you've never had a women's Bible study at your church, we are especially excited for you. Trust me, you can lead. No one was more sure they would fail then I was. Fifteen years later, I'm still organizing studies. Here are a few tips I've learned along the way.

First, ask God to work in your heart and in the hearts of those who come to the study. Ask God to let his Word be the only Word. After all, we aren't trying to get everyone to listen to us. Rather, the goal is to spend time in God's Word so we know and love him more.

Second, lead with humility. Leaders are servants. We are the ones who arrive early to prepare and stay late to pick up. Ask God to give you a heart like Jesus had as he washed his disciples' feet.

Third, your most important job is to moderate. Hopefully, the application questions will encourage discussion. I love to hear how other sisters apply the Word. Another woman's admission of failure reminds me I'm not the only one to struggle. But not every conversation is edifying. Complaining and bashing those in authority is not only unhelpful; it's sinful. If the conversation turns down that road, it's your job to redirect.

Also, occasionally a troubled woman dominates the conversation with a fairly lengthy and involved story. While there is a place to let a woman "bleed" among sisters, sometimes it's best to suggest moving on, while assuring the woman you would be happy to talk more in-depth with her later. I've found very often, that after the study, others are quick to jump in to comfort and guide the woman.

And finally, don't despair if you think the study didn't go as well as you hoped. Fifteen years in, I can still beat myself up when replaying how a study went. *Why didn't I say that? Why did I say that?!* God knows we're not perfect. When the Bible study is lackluster, I go back to the Lord and admit how much I need him. I repent for thinking I somehow can do it on my own, and I pray he'll make the next study better. Any time in the Word is better than no time in the Word. And I guarantee, those of us who lead are notoriously harder on ourselves than those who attend.

Thank you for leading. God is with you, and your sisters in Christ are cheering you on.

Amber Albee Swenson
Project manager

Get to know the ladies who contributed to this book

(their bios appear in the order of the chapters they wrote):

Amber Albee Swenson is a creative writing/literature major who has authored four full-length books and two mini-books. She blogs for Time of Grace and speaks to women with the intent of bringing the Bible to life in tangible, applicable ways. The biggest slice of her life is as mom to four children (ages 19, 17, 14, 11) and wife to her hilarious and heroic but imperfect husband.

Dr. Rhoda Wolle is an educational psychologist who works with schools, faculties, and parents throughout the United States, Asia, and Africa. She serves as the Dean of Student Success at Wisconsin Lutheran College and is an Associate Professor of Education, teaching at both the undergraduate and graduate levels. In her free time she enjoys golfing, sailing, music, reading, and walks on the shore of Lake Michigan with her beagle-mix, Kipper.

Mollie Schairer is a writer, Bible study leader, and stay-at-home mom of three young girls. She is privileged to serve on the WELS Women's Ministry Development Team, which creates Bible studies, devotions, and other resources for the spiritual growth of women. She and her family live in rural Michigan.

Ann M. Ponath lives and writes in beautiful Stillwater, Minnesota. There she and her husband, David, parent four wonderful blessings: David, Christian, Elsa, and Madelyn. Since graduating from Dr. Martin Luther College in 1991, Ann has served as a music and English teacher, church music coordinator, and organist at Christ Lutheran Church and School in North St. Paul, Minnesota.

Naomi Schmidt is a lifetime student of the Word who loves connecting women with Scripture to help them apply Christ-centered truths with meaning and relevance. She enjoys encouraging women as she speaks at events, and she recently published a personal and group Bible study, *Ruth—Living in God's Unfailing Faithfulness*. Naomi and her husband have been blessed with 4 daughters and enjoy spending time with their 8 grandchildren.

Katie Martin lives in Jefferson, Wisconsin with her husband and their four children (ages 20, 18, 13, and 5) who have required them to make Target runs for diapers and dorm room supplies on the same day. She is a 1st and 2nd grade teacher, a Bible study leader, and a writer whose first book, *Cherished Gifts*, was published in 2013. Her passions are helping families grow in Christ, writing, and traveling the world.

Love

Amber Albee Swenson

Definition: *An intense feeling of deep affection; God*

Prayer to open   Heavenly Father, increase our ability to love and serve you. As we lean on you, help us deeply love those we are called to serve. Where there has been hurt, help us forgive. When we are met with hatred, help us to be kind. Increase our love so that we can point the world to you. In Jesus' name we pray. Amen.

Lavish love for God

Love embodies the nine characteristics that comprise the fruit of the Spirit. The other eight stem from love. And no wonder! "God is love" (1 John 4:8). There is no evil, no darkness, no sin found in him.

Lavish love toward God can be expressed in many ways. In the Old Testament, we are given an example of people lavishly loving God through their giving.

Exodus 36:4-7 tells us:

> All the skilled workers who were doing all the work on the sanctuary left what they were doing and said to Moses, "The people are bringing more than enough for doing the work the LORD commanded to be done." Then Moses gave an order and they sent this word throughout the camp: "No man or woman

is to make anything else as an offering for the sanctuary." And so the people were restrained from bringing more, because what they already had was more than enough to do all the work.

Imagine this kind of giving! The children of Israel had to be "restrained" when their gifts outweighed the need. I don't recall ever hearing of that problem. Too often we look at giving in terms of how much we should or have to give instead of seeing it as a privilege.

As the early Christian church grew, when some who had property and land saw their brothers and sisters in Christ in need, they sold their land and property and put the money at the disciples' feet (Acts 4:32-37). They weren't forced or persuaded into giving. Their love for God motivated them to give.

It's easy to love our lavish lifestyle at the expense of giving. When we remember that God is the giver of everything (Psalm 24:1) and that we can't outgive the Giver (Malachi 3:10), we have little reason to hold our money and possessions with clutched hand. I have yet to suffer when spurred to generosity. In fact, I can't think of a time I've missed what I've given to another. I do, however, vividly remember times when others have gone out of their way to be generous to me when I was in need.

Another way we can be lavish in our love for God is through our obedience. When God told Abraham to move, Abraham moved (Genesis 12:1-4). When God told Abraham to let Hagar and Ishmael go, Abraham let them go (Genesis 21:12-14). Even when God asked him to sacrifice his only son, whom he had waited for and loved, Abraham obeyed. God didn't allow him to harm the boy and said to him, "I swear by myself, declares the LORD, that because you have done this and have not withheld your son, your only son, I will surely bless you. . . . Your descendants will take possession of the cities of their enemies, and through your offspring all nations on earth will be blessed, *because you have obeyed me*" (Genesis 22:16-18, emphasis mine).

I'm not always so obedient, and certainly not with the right attitude. Abraham didn't wager with God. He didn't remind God how long he waited for Isaac. Abraham obeyed. Too often I obey grudgingly. I do what I have to do because I have to do it, but I don't hide my displeasure. Obedience to God and those he puts over us is a wonderful way to show our love to God.

Service to God is another way we show our love. Matthew reports that at Jesus' crucifixion, "Many women were there, watching from a distance. They had followed Jesus from Galilee to care for his needs" (Matthew 27:55). "They followed Jesus" implies they left a myriad of other things they could

Love

have been doing to follow and care for Jesus. Their love for Jesus outweighed their love for earthly things, and they gave their effort and time to him.

Their love for Jesus outweighed their love for earthly things, and they gave their effort and time to him.

I easily fall prey to distraction. I get sucked into social media or a Netflix series I shouldn't take the time to watch. How wonderful it must have been to follow Jesus. He never fell into those traps but rather followed God's will with unobstructed focus. I need that same focus in order to serve God to the best of my ability with the time I am given.

We can lavishly love God by living lives of continual worship and prayer like Anna. Luke tells us, "There was also a prophet, Anna, the daughter of Penuel, of the tribe of Asher. . . . She never left the temple but worshiped night and day, fasting and praying" (Luke 2:36,37).

We don't have to live in the temple to live in continual worship. We can worship God throughout our day wherever we are. We do this when "whatever [we] do, in word or deed, [we] do it all in the name of the Lord Jesus, giving thanks to God the Father through him" (Colossians 3:17). Our lives are acts of worship when we do what we do to the best of our ability, with the strength God provides, and with our heart and mind set to honor God.

And, oh, how we need people in prayer! The apostle Paul advised, "Pray in the Spirit on all occasions with all kinds of prayers and requests. With this in mind, be alert and always keep on praying for all the Lord's people" (Ephesians 6:18).

While these efforts are unseen by the church, the effects are certainly felt. God hears and answers our prayers. In response to your prayers, he may intervene to keep a young person from straying, to keep your pastor from despair, to protect leadership from going in the wrong direction, or to provide strength to the missionary. A prayer warrior props up many frontline warriors. Their service, though unseen, is of great value and significance to the kingdom.

Whatever our expression of lavish love, God only wants us to give out of love. God does not want our gifts or service to be given under compulsion or grudgingly (see what God told Cain in Genesis 4:3-7). He doesn't want our acts done for our own glory (see the account of Ananias and Saphira in Acts chapter 5). And obedience with a wayward heart is not obedience. Theologian Charles Spurgeon once wrote, "That obedience which is not voluntary is disobedience, for the Lord looks at the heart, and if he sees that we serve him by compulsion, and not because we love him, he will reject our offering."[1]

The apostle Paul explains it this way: "If I speak in the tongues of men or of angels, but do not have love, I am only a resounding gong or a clanging cymbal. If I have the gift of prophecy and can fathom all mysteries and all knowledge, and if I have a faith that can move mountains, but do not have love, I am nothing. If I give all I possess to the poor and give over my body to hardship that I may boast, but do not have love, I gain nothing" (1 Corinthians 13:1-3).

I don't want to be a clanging cymbal. I don't want my works to fall flat. I certainly don't want to have my efforts wasted. So Lord, increase my love!

Application/Discussion

1. What traits and attributes are we going to need if we are determined to show lavish love for God?

2. Obedience matters to God, not just in the big things but in the little things too. Jesus said, "Whoever can be trusted with very little can also be trusted with much, and whoever is dishonest with very little will also be dishonest with much" (Luke 16:10). Are there some "little things" you need to work on, things like obeying the speed limit or using company time to do your own things when you could and should be doing something at work? How could seeing these things as an expression of love to God motivate you?

3. How else can we express our love for God?

---

[1] Charles H. Spurgeon, *Charles Spurgeon's Morning and Evening* (Green Forest, AR: New Leaf Publishing Group, 2010), January 9, evening.

Love

Loving others lavishly

In Acts chapter 9, Luke writes:

> In Joppa there was a disciple named Tabitha (in Greek her name is Dorcas); she was always doing good and helping the poor. About that time she became sick and died, and her body was washed and placed in an upstairs room. Lydda was near Joppa; so when the disciples heard that Peter was in Lydda, they sent two men to him and urged him, "Please come at once!"
>
> Peter went with them, and when he arrived he was taken upstairs to the room. All the widows stood around him, crying and showing him the robes and other clothing that Dorcas had made while she was still with them. (Acts 9:36-39)

For Tabitha, helping others was not something that happened *on occasion*. She was "always doing good and helping the poor." Love for God manifested itself in love for those around her, especially those she saw who were in need. No doubt she could have used her talents for personal gain. She might have made clothing to sell. She might even have used a portion of the money to give to the poor so they could buy their own clothes. She chose instead to invest in those who had few alternatives.

James tells us: "Suppose a brother or a sister is without clothes and daily food. If one of you says to them, 'Go in peace; keep warm and well fed,' but does nothing about their physical needs, what good is it? In the same way, faith by itself, if it is not accompanied by action, is dead" (James 2:15-17).

Too often, selfishness controls my actions. I'd prefer not to see the needs of those around me; I'd prefer to stay focused on my world, my family, and my issues, shutting myself off to the rest of the world. *Find someone else, Lord,* is too often the honest cry of my soul.

Tabitha shows us what it looks like to respond to needs with, "Here I am, Lord. Use me." Her lavish love for others made such an impact that when she died it wasn't just the widows and the poor but also the disciples who pled her case before Peter and, ultimately, the Lord.

How can we get that kind of love? First, we need to recognize that it's important to God. When one of the Pharisees asked Jesus, "Teacher, which is the greatest commandment?" (Matthew 22:36), Jesus replied, "'Love the Lord your God with all your heart and with all your soul and with all your mind.' This is the first and greatest commandment. And the second is like it: 'Love your neighbor as yourself.' All the Law and the Prophets hang on these two commandments" (Matthew 22:37-40).

The whole of Scripture comes down to realizing that God sent his Son to die for us, not because we were worthy but because of his love. When that truth penetrates our soul, we are prepared for service to others. God asks us to have that same love for others, regardless of how they respond and regardless of whether we feel they are worthy.

Jesus said, "You have heard that it was said, 'Love your neighbor and hate your enemy.' But I tell you, love your enemies and pray for those who persecute you, that you may be children of your Father in heaven. He causes his sun to rise on the evil and the good, and sends rain on the righteous and the unrighteous" (Matthew 5:43-45).

God calls us, his children, to be different. While the rest of the world strives to gather and store more and to use time in a self absorbed, self-serving manner, we are to stand apart because we have tasted God's love. In turn, we should readily give that love to others. I can't sew, so I won't be making clothes for anyone, but I can make meals, and I often serve other people's children at my house. You may not be so inclined to watch people's children, but you might be in a position to visit shut-ins or to drive an elderly friend to a clinic appointment. The particulars are not nearly as important as recognizing and filling a need with love.

> *While the rest of the world strives to gather and store more and to use time in a self-absorbed, self-serving manner, we are to stand apart because we have tasted God's love, and, in turn, readily give that love to others.*

Once, when John the Baptist was calling the people to repentance, he said, "Anyone who has two shirts should share with the one who has none, and anyone who has food should do the same" (Luke 3:11).

Part of being motivated to lavishly love others is admitting God has given me enough and he has equipped me to readily and cheerfully share with those who are not so fortunate. Our love for God causes us to bless others instead of using everything to live lavishly for ourselves.

Application/Discussion

4. In the Western world, we have so much stuff that it can be hard to identify a need. We struggle to find the right gift to give someone for their birthday or Christmas because everyone has so much. It's important for us to understand that the significant need of another

Love

may not be a physical thing. What else might people long for other than things? What might you do to fill those needs?

5. The hardest part of being the solution to someone's need may be giving something up. To be a friend to the lonely person at my child's school may mean not sitting by my best friend at the basketball game, but instead sitting by the person who otherwise would be sitting alone. It may require that I notice the new person at church and make the effort to find out who that person is. What things are required for us to start loving others lavishly?

6. As I mentioned above, sometimes we have to give up something we like or love for the sake of fulfilling the needs of someone else. I may need to give up time in front of the TV to attend to the neighborhood kids who flock to my house. I may need to give up or significantly reduce the time I spend on a hobby that has no eternal value in order to spend it on something that does. What time-stealers might you give up in order to make a greater impact in God's kingdom? Are you willing to do that?

Loving like Jesus

If we want to see love in action, we look at Jesus. He was and is love. Look at how he interacted with the Samaritan woman at the well.

"Now [Jesus] had to go through Samaria. So he came to a town in Samaria called Sychar, near the plot of ground Jacob had given to his son Joseph. Jacob's well was there, and Jesus, tired as he was from the journey, sat down by the well. It was about noon" (John 4:4-6).

Here we notice that Christ showed his love by obedience. He "had to go through Samaria" because his Father willed it. It wasn't the easy or preferred route. In fact, most Jews went around Samaria because of the deep-seated rifts between Jews and Samaritans that went back generations.[2]

Obedience is an important part of love. Jesus told his disciples and us, "If you love me, keep my commands" (John 14:15). The apostle John reiterated the message later, saying, "In fact, this is love for God: to keep his commands" (1 John 5:3).

Christ's love was not only obedient; it was sacrificial. When Jesus arrived at the well, he was tired. Besides that, it was noon, the hottest part of the day. The next verses tell us the disciples had gone for food, so there's a good chance he was hungry too. How eager are you to help someone, whether or not the gospel is involved, when you are exhausted, hot, and hungry? And who would blame us for neglecting others in those circumstances?

Later, we read: [Jesus] told her, "Go, call your husband and come back."

"I have no husband," she replied.

> *Jesus' love didn't discriminate, and ours shouldn't either.*

Jesus said to her, "You are right when you say you have no husband. The fact is, you have had five husbands, and the man you now have is not your husband. What you have just said is quite true." (John 4:16-18)

This use of the law wasn't meant to cut the woman down but rather to demonstrate her need for the Savior who was there wanting to save her soul. The other women in town might have considered her unworthy of saving. But Jesus' love didn't discriminate, and ours shouldn't either. We all fall short in the morality department, but God still loves us. James reminds us that often the ones who are successful in the eyes of the world treat

---

[2] Concordia self-study Bible, New International Version (St. Louis: Concordia, 1986), p. 1609.
Gary P. Baumler, *John,* The People's Bible Series (Milwaukee: Northwestern Publishing House, 1984), p. 60.

Love

others, especially those who are poor, the worst (James 2:6,7). Our affection should not be reserved for people we consider worthy while we turn up our noses at those shunned by society.

In the next verses it became clear the Samaritan woman's theology was wrong too. Jesus had no problem working with that either. Are we so gracious? Are we willing to work with people who spout half-truths or convoluted truths or who know nothing of the truths of Scripture? Or is it easier to just roll our eyes and talk about "those people"?

Jesus' entire life embodied love. He left the perfection of heaven to be God with us, and he showed us that love is having mercy on the sinner, having compassion for the hurting, and providing for those in need. He showed us that as true God he has power over the forces of nature so that in our fear we know to turn to him. In love he revealed that the way to defeat Satan is with the Word, so we might overcome the devil. In love he showed that ministry is love in action, that we might serve others. And then he showed how great love could be when he willingly allowed himself to be tortured, put on a cross, and forsaken by his Father in order that we might be with him for eternity.

We could easily dismiss all of this because of Jesus' divinity. Of course he could love this way. But, before we excuse ourselves from the difficult work of loving the unlovable, remember Jesus' words the night he was taken captive to suffer and die. He told his disciples: "I have set you an example that you should do as I have done for you. Now that you know these things, you will be blessed if you do them" (John 13:15,17).

Our sinful natures will prevent us from ever being able to love perfectly. But that shouldn't keep us from trying. Through the power of the Holy Spirit and the example of Christ, we have access to all we need in order to love well. But we must stay rooted in Christ to draw nourishment from him (Colossians 2:7). My love often falls short. It is only through prayer and Bible study and the strength God provides that I can love the woman who budges in line at the supermarket, the slightly annoying child who isn't paying attention in class, the people I share my home with, and those I don't know at all.

I'm not sure there is a greater challenge, nor is there anything more worthy of our time and energy. The world is a cruel place. If Christians aren't bearers of love, then who will be? With the help of God, we can follow the example of Christ, get out of our comfort zones, squelch our selfishness, and love those God puts in our paths.

Application/Discussion

7. The more uncomfortable I am, the less inclined I am to think of anyone else. Yet we noted that Jesus was tired, hot, and hungry when he arrived in Samaria and poured his grace into the woman at the well. How do we develop a mindset for unfettered and undeterred service?

8. Jesus offered this challenge:

> "If you love those who love you, what credit is that to you? Even sinners love those who love them. And if you do good to those who are good to you, what credit is that to you? Even sinners do that. And if you lend to those from whom you expect repayment, what credit is that to you? Even sinners lend to sinners, expecting to be repaid in full. But love your enemies, do good to them, and lend to them without expecting to get anything back. Then your reward will be great, and you will be children of the Most High, because he is kind to the ungrateful and wicked." (Luke 6:32-35)

Whom do you struggle to love? (Make a list!) This is now your prayer list. Pray that God might help you love those people well that they might see Christ in you.

Love

Key takeaways

- Lavish love for God can manifest itself in many ways. Some include: obedience, offerings, worship, and service.

- Love for God motivates us to use what we have for his kingdom.

- Lavish love for others motivates us to look to the needs of others rather than to store up more for ourselves.

- Christ's love was obedient, sacrificial, indiscriminating, grace-filled, merciful, and kind.

- If I want abundant love in my life, I need to be rooted in Jesus through Bible study and prayer.

Prayer to close Heavenly Father, increase my love! My love wears thin and too often my heart grows cold. Warm me with your love, that I might be a source of love to others. Let all I do point the world to you. In Jesus' name I pray. Amen.

Joy

Dr. Rhoda Wolle

Definition: *An ongoing state of mind that incorporates contentment, peace, and being filled with gratitude despite life's circumstances.*

Prayer to open   Heavenly Father, I long to have the joy that only you can give. Please quiet my heart as I spend time focusing on you. Teach me your ways. Draw me closer to you, and grant that your will is my will. Help me be grateful for all the blessings you have given me, most of all, for salvation through my Savior, Jesus. Let this knowledge grant me that peace that passes all understanding, and instill in me unshakable joy that praises and trusts in you regardless of my circumstances. In your Son's name I pray and trust that you hear me. Amen.

How do I become joyful?

You're ready to give birth. It's your first child. With great anticipation, you look forward to meeting this little one face-to-face. When the time comes, you give birth in a stable. Mary must have been disappointed with her circumstances, yet she said, "My soul glorifies the Lord and my spirit rejoices in God my Savior" (Luke 1:46,47).

Joy

Constantly chained to a soldier, unable to move about as you please, you are frustrated. Yet even after enduring months of such imprisonment, Paul encouraged the church in Philippi, and helped them understand that God used his time of imprisonment to spread the gospel. That thought brought him unshakable joy.

"I thank my God every time I remember you. In all my prayers for all of you, I always pray with joy because of your partnership in the gospel from the first day until now, being confident of this, that he who began a good work in you will carry it on to completion until the day of Christ Jesus.

It is right for me to feel this way about all of you, since I have you in my heart and, whether I am in chains or defending and confirming the gospel, all of you share in God's grace with me. God can testify how I long for all of you with the affection of Christ Jesus.

And this is my prayer: that your love may abound more and more in knowledge and depth of insight, so that you may be able to discern what is best and may be pure and blameless for the day of Christ, filled with the fruit of righteousness that comes through Jesus Christ—to the glory and praise of God.

Now I want you to know, brothers and sisters, that what has happened to me has actually served to advance the gospel. As a result, it has become clear throughout the whole palace guard and to everyone else that I am in chains for Christ. And because of my chains, most of the brothers and sisters have become confident in the Lord and dare all the more to proclaim the gospel without fear." (Philippians 1:3-14)

Joy is not dependent upon our circumstances. Time and again the Scriptures remind us that we can be joyful regardless of what is happening around us. How do we find joy like this? Let's explore this concept together. But first, what is joy?

Some people equate happiness with joy. *Merriam-Webster* defines happiness as a "state of well-being; a pleasurable or satisfying experience," while a definition for joy includes "the emotion evoked by well-being, success, or good fortune or by the prospect of possessing what one desires."[3]

---

[3] *Merriam-Webster* online dictionary: https://www.merriam-webster.com/dictionary/happiness and https://www.merriam-webster.com/dictionary/joy, accessed January 2019.

In God's Orchard

Instead of discussing how they are different, let's consider how happiness and joy are connected. Scripture speaks of both. It varies by translation, but the Bible uses the words *happy* or *happiness* over 30 times and *joy* and *rejoice* appear over 300 times.

Let's think of joy as an ongoing state of mind that incorporates contentment, peace, and being filled with gratitude despite life's circumstances. It's embodied in the words of Isaiah 35:10: "Those the LORD has rescued will return. They will enter Zion with singing; everlasting joy will crown their heads. Gladness and joy will overtake them, and sorrow and sighing will flee away."

Where does joy like this come from? The key to understanding and having joy is God's Spirit. Joy is a fruit of the Spirit. As we stay connected to the vine, joy is a byproduct, or fruit, that flows from that connection. The apostle John explains, "I am the vine; you are the branches. If you remain in me and I in you, you will bear much fruit; apart from me you can do nothing" (John 15:5).

How do we stay connected to the vine and experience this wondrous joy regardless of life's circumstances? The writer of Hebrews suggests we remember that these circumstances are temporary. "You suffered along with those in prison and joyfully accepted the confiscation of your property, because you knew that you yourselves had better and lasting possessions" (Hebrews 10:34). He reminds the same group of believers that Jesus, knowing the outcome, found joy amidst humiliation. "The joy set before him he endured the cross, scorning its shame, and sat down at the right hand of the throne of God" (Hebrews 12:2).

We can find joy regardless of the pain or discomfort we experience in our here and now because these present sufferings are not only temporary; they "are not worth comparing with the glory that will be revealed in us" (Romans 8:18).

Christians know our time on earth, however difficult, does not compare to the wonders we will enjoy for eternity in heaven.

Christians know our time on earth, however difficult, does not compare to the wonders we will enjoy for eternity in heaven.

When we struggle to remember that, we can follow the apostle Peter's advice: "Grow in the grace and knowledge of our Lord and Savior Jesus Christ" (2 Peter 3:18). Every day you and I fall short of the perfect and beautiful plan God has for us. Yet we know that no matter how much we mess up, we have a fresh start through repentance and forgiveness.

Joy

Psalm 103 reminds us, "As far as the east is from the west, so far has he removed our transgressions from us" (verse 12). If we confess a sin, the burden of that sin is lifted from us, placed on Jesus, and resolved at the cross. We no longer carry that burden. It is gone forever.

This is a reason for great joy! "Blessed is the one whose transgressions are forgiven, whose sins are covered" (Psalm 32:1).

And when we struggle, we can join Paul in asking the question,

Who shall separate us from the love of Christ? Shall trouble or hardship or persecution or famine or nakedness or danger or sword? As it is written:

"For your sake we face death all day long; we are considered as sheep to be slaughtered."

No, in all these things we are more than conquerors through him who loved us. For I am convinced that neither death nor life, neither angels nor demons, neither the present nor the future, nor any powers, neither height nor depth, nor anything else in all creation, will be able to separate us from the love of God that is in Christ Jesus our Lord. (Romans 8:35-40)

Application/Discussion

1. Think of times you have been filled with joy. What were you experiencing that brought about joy?

2. Can you remember a time when you were not filled with joy but wished you were?

3. Knowing that joy comes from staying connected to the Word, what can you do to connect when you don't really "feel" joyful?

4. What can we do to support and encourage others when they are lacking joy?

Where joy can and cannot be found

Christians experience joy in many contexts. Consider these:

We experience joy in our identity as adopted sons and daughters of the King who are now part of his royal priesthood. Many people desire time with royalty. We have instant and continual access to the King of all creation. No matter what happens in life, one plus God is a majority. We are on the winning side. We know how it all turns out. This brings a lasting sense of peace and joy. "The kingdom of God is not a matter of eating and drinking, but of righteousness, peace and joy in the Holy Spirit" (Romans 14:17).

We experience happiness in time spent with family, friends, and fellow believers. When we are with people we love and who love us, there is laughter in good times and empathy and understanding in challenging times. We reap joy when, together, we grow in the Word. We build one another up and encourage one another and carry one another's burdens. "We work with you for your joy" (2 Corinthians 1:24).

Worshiping ignites joy. Have you ever been sitting in church and the pastor's message gives you a sense of complete peace, or a hymn encourages and edifies you so that you feel your chest might burst? Have you heard another Christian speak of a struggle and all of a sudden you realize you aren't alone in your struggle? We comprehend the joy that drew the psalmist to the Lord's house. "I rejoiced with those who said to me, 'Let us go to the house of the LORD'" (Psalm 122:1).

When we follow God's commands, blessings often follow, which bring joy.

When we follow God's commands, blessings often follow, which bring joy. Psalm 1:1-3 tells us of the blessings of the person " . . . whose delight is in the law of the Lord, and who meditates on his law day and night. . . ." Hebrews 1:9 reiterates, "You have loved righteousness and hated wickedness; therefore God, your God, has set you above your companions by anointing you with the oil of joy." Jesus

16

encourages us, "If you keep my commands, you will remain in my love, just as I have kept my Father's commands and remain in his love. I have told you this so that my joy may be in you and that your joy may be complete" (John 15:10,11). As we find strength in his Word and sacrament, we live in his will for our lives. This is where that complete joy is found.

And what can steal our joy? Sometimes we mistake pleasure for joy. Joy comes from being connected to God, whereas pleasure comes from things in the world. Too much pleasure has the potential to steal our joy. When we look for joy in a new job, house, or car, or from food, alcohol, or relationships, we may experience pleasure; but pleasure is fleeting. Blessings certainly add to our pleasure, but pleasure can't be confused with authentic, unshakable joy found in our relationship with God, because joy survives even when the pleasure fades.

King Solomon sought pleasure through earthly blessings to replace the joy found only in the Lord. He looked for meaning and joy in wisdom, in relationships, in work, and in earthly pleasures. "I denied myself nothing my eyes desired; I refused my heart no pleasure. My heart took delight in all my labor, and this was the reward for all my toil. Yet when I surveyed all that my hands had done and what I had toiled to achieve, everything was meaningless, a chasing after the wind; nothing was gained under the sun" (Ecclesiastes 2:10,11).

The wisest man to ever live concluded that all of these earthly pursuits are not where we find meaning or joy. Rather, we find meaning knowing that God is in control, and we can trust him. Because of this, we are able to enjoy what he gives us while on earth. "So I commend the enjoyment of life, because there is nothing better for a person under the sun than to eat and drink and be glad. Then joy will accompany them in their toil all the days of the life God has given them under the sun" (Ecclesiastes 8:15).

Application/Discussion

5. In which context of walking with God listed above do you find great joy?

6. What "blessings" have you mistakenly considered to be a source of joy?

7. Does being a member of the family of believers; repenting of sins; and worshipping God, both in his house and by dedicating your heart and actions to him, bring you joy? Do some of these things bring more joy than others? Why do you think that is?

The profound truth that can bring you and me unending joy is this: Jesus already took care of all of the really difficult things.

8. Amidst all the distractions of life, how can we keep from becoming sidelined by pleasures in order to maintain our primary focus on the source of joy, rather than the blessings?

Jesus is our joy

If you are concerned or worried that you don't have enough joy, or that you aren't joyful in all circumstances, rest assured it is not about you or your strength; Jesus makes our joy complete. Jesus led a life of constant communion with his Father: When he was a boy of 12 in the temple, when

Joy

he was celebrating a friend's wedding and making more wine, when he was surrounded by smiling children who wanted to sit on his knee and walk on the tops of his feet. He fulfilled every requirement to pay the price for our sin. The profound truth that can bring you and me unending joy is this: Jesus already took care of all of the really difficult things. Now we live a life of love and gratitude for what he has already done for us.

This infused joy—which is ours in Jesus, which results from knowing what he has done for us, which recognizes that every good gift is from above—enables us to experience many blessings.

How can we not be grateful when we see all of the blessings we have been given?

I learned a wonderful lesson from a woman working at the department of motor vehicles (DMV). The DMV does not have the same reputation as Disney World. People don't get excited to go there and wait in lines. It's not what we consider a cheerful place. I was there around 2 P.M. After waiting in line, I got up to the window and asked the woman working behind the counter how she was. She replied, "I am too blessed to be stressed!" Isn't that a beautiful thought?

I attempt to remind myself daily that someone right now is praying for something I am taking for granted. Someone woke up this morning with legs that don't work, longing for the ability to get out of bed and walk across the room. Someone is praying for a meal to soothe their hungry, aching stomach. Someone is walking four miles to a dirty watering hole to gather water for her family while I go to the sink and with the turn of a faucet get clear, clean, drinkable water. Someone right now is praying for a job, and for a warm, dry bed to sleep in tonight. Someone is praying for the love of a family. Many across the world are praying for peace from the ravages of ongoing warfare. People are praying for peace that comes from not being afraid of their eternal fate. You and I have so much to be grateful for. With joy rooted in Christ, we can develop a habit of counting our blessings instead of our worries.

I was born and raised in Arizona. Though I have lived in the Midwest for over 20 years, I still don't enjoy snow. And yet I have dear friends who do. They find all kinds of good things to say about it, things like: a fresh snowfall coating the ground is so peaceful; when it is snowing, I get to wear warm cozy sweaters and sit inside and read a book and drink coffee; I can play in the snow and make snowmen and snow angels; I enjoy cross-country skiing. Basically, they are seeing the good that comes with the snowfall, while I focus on what I don't like: driving in it, the gray sky, having to wear a jacket. We usually find what we look for. If we look for the positives, we will find them; whereas, if we look for the negatives, we will find them. God, the giver of all good things, has put something to be grateful for in every season. When the sun shines on a spring day and the birds happily chirp, we recognize the blessing. But we can also recognize the blessing and beauty in the falling leaves of autumn and in the fresh blanket of winter snow.

We have a choice in how we think about gratitude. While there are many things in life that are out of our control, we have control over the thoughts we allow to linger in our minds. If a thought is not serving you well, you are able to replace it with a different thought. In neuroscience this ability is called neuroplasticity. As we think a thought over and over, we develop a neural pathway, a habit of thought, or a memory. As we change the thoughts we think over and over, we develop new neural pathways, or new habits of thought. The choice is ours. We choose if we want to be grateful.

I often think of the Israelites as they wandered in the desert for 40 years prior to entering the Promised Land. God took care of all their needs. God gave them victory over their enemies when they were attacked and provided for their safe passage. He gave them sandals that never wore out. He provided food in the form of manna and quail. They had clean water to drink. And by means of a pillar that always went before them, he showed them the path they were to take. They could have chosen to be overwhelmed with gratitude that he was with them and guiding them to the Promised Land while providing all their needs along the way, or they could have chosen to grumble. You and I have that same choice every day.

We know from Scripture that our joy radiates to others. God had given his chosen people a set of regulations that were supposed to be a blessing to them and make them a shining beacon to the world. As God's chosen people followed his will and received his blessings, peoples from all around them would be drawn to them. King Solomon asked for the gift of wisdom, and God granted his request. His fame spread throughout the world. As King Solomon's fame spread, the queen of Sheba traveled from Africa to see him and experience his wisdom.

> When the queen of Sheba heard about the fame of Solomon and his relationship to the LORD, she came to test Solomon with hard questions. Arriving at Jerusalem with a very great caravan—with camels carrying spices, large quantities of gold, and precious stones—she came to Solomon and talked with him

Joy

about all that she had on her mind. Solomon answered all her questions; nothing was too hard for the king to explain to her. When the queen of Sheba saw all the wisdom of Solomon and the palace he had built, the food on his table, the seating of his officials, the attending servants in their robes, his cupbearers, and the burnt offerings he made at the temple of the Lord, she was overwhelmed.

She said to the king, "The report I heard in my own country about your achievements and your wisdom is true. But I did not believe these things until I came and saw with my own eyes. Indeed, not even half was told me; in wisdom and wealth you have far exceeded the report I heard. How happy your people must be! How happy your officials, who continually stand before you and hear your wisdom! Praise be to the Lord your God, who has delighted in you and placed you on the throne of Israel. Because of the Lord's eternal love for Israel, he has made you king to maintain justice and righteousness." (1 Kings 10:1-9)

As King Solomon faithfully served the Lord and his people, he had joy. That joy was a light to those who didn't believe. It made others curious. God gives this same opportunity to you and me. As we worship our Lord and live our lives in joy, according to his will, we are a beacon to a hurting world.

The world longs for the fruit of the spirit. People around you are looking for love, joy, peace, patience, kindness, goodness, faithfulness, gentleness, and self-control. They are often looking for it in things of this earth. You and I get to witness about the source of our joy and to share that joy with those who long for it. "May the God of hope fill you with all joy and peace as you trust in him, so that you may overflow with hope by the power of the Holy Spirit" (Romans 15:13). We do not need to *do* anything to have joy. As we spend time in the Word, the Holy Spirit does the work in our hearts that brings us joy. It's all about him and what he has done. Joy looks upward, not inward. "The joy of the Lord is your strength" (Nehemiah 8:10).

Shalom is a Hebrew word used by God's people as both a greeting similar to "hello" and also as the parting thought of "goodbye." *Shalom* incorporates the concepts of peace, harmony, completeness, wellness, prosperity, welfare, and calmness. One beautiful word contains all of these wishes. You and I are God's chosen people, and we have *shalom* because we have been reconciled through Christ. "God was pleased to have all his fullness dwell in him, and through him to reconcile to himself all things, whether things on earth or things in heaven, by making peace through his blood, shed on the cross" (Colossians 1:19,20).

Because of what Jesus did for you and me, we are at peace. We can experience true, lasting, unshakable joy. *Shalom!*

Application/Discussion

9. It is so tempting to depend on our own resources. If we look inward, we will not find joy. Joy is found by looking upward, to our heavenly Father who provides all good things. What can you do to constantly remind yourself and those around you of where true and lasting joy comes from?

10. What does the concept of *shalom* mean to you? What is the aspect of shalom that you find most intriguing and appealing? Is it yours today? Why or why not?

Key takeaways

- Joy is not dependent on our circumstances.

- Authentic joy comes from staying connected to God through time spent in his Word.

- As we enjoy this unshakable joy, we will experience many blessings.

- Blessings and pleasures are not the source of our joy.

Joy

- Joy is not of our own doing. We don't look inward if we don't have it or have enough of it. Jesus earned it for us. Stay connected to him and joy will flow.

- We always have a choice. We can be grateful, or we can grumble.

- Joy is ours because of the redeeming work of our Savior. *Shalom!*

Prayer to close

Holy Spirit, thank you for being the conduit for my joy. No matter what I do, or how I fail, or what I experience in life, I can be filled with joy because of you and because of what Jesus has done. Always redirect my thoughts toward you. Please fill me with the joy that can only be found in you. When I have the choice to be grateful or grumble, redirect my heart. Give me a grateful heart filled with joy so that I can live a life of worship and so that others will see your joy in me and long for the same. Nothing is impossible for you. Your spirit is joy. Please continue to fill me with that same spirit. I trust that you will because I ask this in Jesus' name, and I know that you hear me. Amen.

Peace

Amber Albee Swenson

Definition: *Order, harmony, calm, tranquility*

Prayer to open   O God, so often my life is anything but peaceful. Help me to know and relish your peace, a peace that calls me to endure difficult situations with quietness and trust. Help me to relinquish worry and to put on noble strength instead. Help me to discern when it is time to walk away from a situation and when it is better to stay and submit. In a world of discord, let me be a peacemaker. Through Jesus, my Redeemer I pray. Amen.

Submitting for the sake of peace

Genesis chapter 13 tells of an issue that arose between Abram and his nephew Lot. This is what we're told:

> Now Lot, who was moving about with Abram, also had flocks and herds and tents. But the land could not support them while they stayed together, for their possessions were so great that they were not able to stay together. And quarreling arose between Abram's herders and Lot's. The Canaanites and Perizzites were also living in the land at that time.

Peace

So Abram said to Lot, "Let's not have any quarreling between you and me, or between your herders and mine, for we are close relatives. Is not the whole land before you? Let's part company. If you go to the left, I'll go to the right; if you go to the right, I'll go to the left."

Lot looked around and saw that the whole plain of the Jordan toward Zoar was well watered, like the garden of the LORD, like the land of Egypt. (This was before the LORD destroyed Sodom and Gomorrah.) So Lot chose for himself the whole plain of the Jordan and set out toward the east. The two men parted company: Abram lived in the land of Canaan, while Lot lived among the cities of the plain and pitched his tents near Sodom. (Genesis 13:5-12)

Due to the Lord's abundant blessing and an increase of flocks and herds as well as servants and possessions, it became problematic for Abram and his nephew to remain in close quarters. Abram refused to let this issue be the downfall of the relationship.

Though he was older and held the place of authority, Abram allowed Lot to take his pick of the land. Abram rightly realized the increase they were experiencing was from God. If God was with Abram, his blessing would be upon him whether he pitched his tent to the east or west, north or south. Abram chose the path of submission for the sake of peace.

If you're a people pleaser, this may be your natural tendency. The rest of us will have to work at it. It is all too easy to go to war over things that don't really matter and/or lose sight of the fact that God controls everything. All too often I realize this only after throwing a tantrum. There's a good chance that if I had been in Abram's position, I might have said, "Why do you think you should have the best land?"

> *O Lord, help us to be more like Abram and to submit for the sake of peace, knowing your watchful eyes see the sacrifice.*

This attitude pops up in marriage when we decide not to do the dishes because we've done them the rest of the week. Or when we gladly help the children pick up but refuse to help our spouse with his mess. It happens when we deliberately avoid the e-mail calling for volunteers because it's time others pull their weight. It happens when we keep score among siblings regarding who has done what for Mom or Dad. O Lord, help us to be more like Abram and to submit for the sake of peace, knowing your watchful eyes see the sacrifice.

In God's Orchard

If we were to read on in Genesis, we'd find that in the end Abram was better off. Lot looked at the land and chose what appealed to him. He saw lush land with plenty of water but failed to notice the wickedness of the environment.

How often don't we fall for the same scheme? We can be tricked into choosing a place of peace that is not spiritually safe. We may be drawn by charisma, charm, wit, or the amazing production of a TV show or movie. We can be sucked in by the appearance or attention of another person. But if the plot of the show or the character of that person is morally corrupt, we endanger our own character by giving our time to it or him or her. Little by little, usually without even realizing, our morality erodes.

We may find it very peaceful in the house when everyone's gaze is glued to the screens of their devices. But is that the best option? Are the concepts and beliefs that are filtering into our minds for our spiritual good? As the apostle Paul wrote, "Do not be misled: 'Bad company corrupts good character'" (1 Corinthians 15:33). Our eyes and senses aren't to take the lead when making decisions, but instead we follow God's guidance as we study Scripture, pray, and seek the advice of trusted believers. We don't want to be unaware of Satan's attempts to lead us astray. The apostle Peter warns, "Be alert and of sober mind. Your enemy the devil prowls around like a roaring lion looking for someone to devour" (1 Peter 5:8).

When we find ourselves in a situation which requires that we submit for the sake of peace—and in doing so, we get the short end of the stick—we, like Abram, can put the situation into God's capable hands. God sees our heart and will bless our willful submission for the benefit of others.

Even Jesus submitted for the sake of peace. In the Garden of Gethsemane, Jesus asked the Father to take the cup of suffering from him. God the Father said no, but he sent an angel to strengthen Jesus (Luke 22:43). Before Pilate, Jesus refused to speak in his defense and submitted to being condemned to death on a cross. Jesus' willingness to be mistreated and to submit resulted in our eternal peace. That peace is our motivation to do the same.

Application/Discussion

1. On his last night on earth with his disciples, Jesus purposefully took the lowliest position and washed his disciples' feet. Often we will have to give up our "rights" to having first choice or getting equal shares or top priority if we want peace. Read these words from John 13:3: "Jesus knew that the Father had put all things under his

power, and that he had come from God and was returning to God."
What significant thoughts do you see in this verse?

2. Jesus went on to say, "Now that I, your Lord and Teacher, have
washed your feet, you also should wash one another's feet. I have
set you an example that you should do as I have done for you"
(John 13:14,15). Of all Jesus could have said on his last night with
his disciples, this was of high priority. Why do you think it is so
important for us to understand the concept of submitting for the
sake of peace?

Years ago an older woman taught me a valuable lesson. Her
parents had helped her two brothers out financially. They offered
her the same amount of money. She refused, telling her parents
God had provided for all her needs and she didn't need their money.
Instead of taking the money, she told her parents she was grateful
they had been in a position to help her brothers.

That's been a great lesson for me to keep in mind. There were times
my children didn't get the same amount of time with my parents as
other grandchildren. There were things my siblings inherited from
other relatives. This woman taught me to refrain from keeping score
or feeling jilted and to instead look to God for all I need.

3. How can grabbing hold of this concept impact our outlook on
submitting for the sake of peace?

4. Look at these passages. What basic truths will keep us from feeling
jilted when others are blessed in ways we aren't?
a. Matthew 6:26,27: "Look at the birds of the air; they do not sow
or reap or store away in barns, and yet your heavenly Father feeds

them. Are you not much more valuable than they? Can any one of you by worrying add a single hour to your life?"

b. Psalm 37:5,6: "Commit your way to the LORD; trust in him and he will do this: He will make your righteous reward shine like the dawn, your vindication like the noonday sun."

c. 1 Peter 5:6: "Humble yourselves, therefore, under God's mighty hand, that he may lift you up in due time."

Separating for the sake of peace

In the book of 1 Samuel, David confronted his good friend Jonathon with the idea that Jonathon's father, King Saul, was trying to kill David. Jonathon didn't believe it. He thought that if his dad were plotting to kill David, he would tell him first. Jonathon was wrong. David and Jonathon devised a way to see what was in Saul's heart, and when it came out that Saul indeed had in mind to kill David, they decided it was best for David to leave. We're told:

David got up from the south side of the stone and bowed down before Jonathan three times, with his face to the ground. Then they kissed each other and wept together—but David wept the most.

Jonathan said to David, "Go in peace, for we have sworn friendship with each other in the name of the LORD, saying, 'The LORD is witness between you and me, and between your descendants and my descendants forever.'" Then David left, and Jonathan went back to the town." (1 Samuel 20:41,42)

Sometimes the only way to have peace is to remove yourself from a situation. David had to leave Saul's presence because Saul was determined to

Peace

kill him. Walking away wasn't his first course of action. He had remained in and out of Saul's court for 15 or 16 years and had escaped several attempts (1 Samuel 18:11; 19:10) on his life before he came to that decision.

The apostle Paul said in the book of Romans, "If it is possible, as far as it depends on you, live at peace with everyone" (12:18). "If it is possible" suggests parting ways is not the first plan. The first priority is always to love beyond what is reasonable and to submit as our Lord Jesus himself did. Followers of Christ are not to be inconsiderate or without compassion. We're not to keep score or storm out of a situation if we don't get our way.

> *The first priority is always to love beyond what is reasonable and to submit as our Lord Jesus himself did.*

However, like for David, there are times peace is unattainable through no fault of our own. Even after David finally removed himself from Saul, Saul chased him for years trying to kill him.

In the book of Genesis, we're told of the young Joseph, so hated by his brothers that they sold him into slavery to get rid of him. This separation resulted when his older brother Judah came up with the idea to sell Joseph rather than to kill him.

Mary and Joseph fled to Egypt to escape Herod who saw young Jesus as a threat that needed to be exterminated. Even after Herod's death, Mary and Joseph settled in Nazareth upon their return, away from Herod's cruel son.

Separation in these examples was a matter of life or death. We likely won't receive death threats, but we may experience hatred to an extent that escape or avoidance is the prudent plan. The separation isn't always permanent. Sometimes hearts soften through the years and the relationship can be restored or repaired.

There are other times when physical separation isn't possible. We can't always move away from an undesirable neighbor. We sometimes have to endure a hostile work environment while waiting for another door to open. We are called to stay in our marriages and work things out.

Only God can give us the wisdom to know when and if it's time to separate for the sake of peace. During turbulent times, it's good to seek God's will through Bible study and prayer and the advice and counsel of godly friends and relatives. If a separation is deemed necessary, it is important to do it with a pure heart.

The account of Paul and Barnabas separating is an example worth consideration. Barnabas had been the first person to take the newly converted

In God's Orchard

Paul under his wing. Together they completed Paul's first missionary journey. When it came time to go out again, we're told:

> Barnabas wanted to take John, also called Mark, with them, but Paul did not think it wise to take him, because he had deserted them in Pamphylia and had not continued with them in the work. They had such a sharp disagreement that they parted company. Barnabas took Mark and sailed for Cyprus, but Paul chose Silas and left, commended by the believers to the grace of the Lord. He went through Syria and Cilicia, strengthening the churches. (Acts 15:37-41)

These two godly men disagreed to the point they deemed separation necessary, and yet God blessed and worked through them both. They even covered twice as much ground! Perhaps even more incredible is the relationship that developed between John Mark and Paul. Paul's last letter, 2 Timothy, records these words: "Do your best to come to me quickly. . . . Only Luke is with me. Get Mark and bring him with you, because he is helpful to me in my ministry" (4:9, 11).

Over the course of the years of separation John Mark had proven himself to be worthy. Though he "deserted" Paul and Barnabas at first, he grew to become a reliable partner in ministry. God worked to soften Paul's heart too. Grudges have no place in the kingdom. Sometimes, time is required to get past the hurt and to a point where two people can work together again.

May the years of separation do exactly that. May God strengthen the weak and soften the strong so that we can join forces against the devil and his army. They are the real enemy, the ones we want far from us.

Application/Discussion

5. How do we discern whether separation is the best option? What should our attitude be when separating from another?

6. Anger and hurt are almost always in the mix when separation occurs. If we don't deal with these things, bitterness creeps in. David wrote

Peace

psalms during his years on the run from Saul. What can we do to deal with bitterness so it doesn't poison our souls?

7. What peacemaking tasks should we be doing in times of separation to work toward peace?

True peace God's way

The night of Jesus' birth, angels appeared in the sky above the shepherds in the fields outside of Bethlehem. The angel of the Lord announced Jesus had been born. Then, "a great company of the heavenly host appeared with the angel, praising God and saying, 'Glory to God in the highest heaven, and on earth peace to those on whom his favor rests'" (Luke 2:13,14).

God opened the sky to announce peace. This eternal peace would not be experienced by all people but by those "on whom his favor rests." God's peace rested on those who, up to that point, looked forward to a day when the Messiah would come to save them from their sins; and after Jesus' death, God's peace rested on those who believed his sacrificial offering was for the redemption of their sins.

Jesus left heaven to give his life as an exchange for ours. He made peace with God on our behalf.

The symbolism of this peace happened the minute Jesus took his last breath. At that time, the curtain in the temple was torn in two. Up until that point, the curtain separated God and man. God's room—the Holy of Holies, or the Most Holy Place—was off limits to everyone but one priest, once a year on the Day of Atonement. On that day, the priest offered the blood of a goat to atone, or pay for, the sin of the people.[4]

Because the blood of animals could never fully pay the price for the people's sin, the ritual had to be done year after year after year. But when Jesus, the perfect sacrificial lamb, paid the price in full, the curtain was torn to indicate the separation of God and man was over.

---

[4] Jerome G. Albrecht, *Matthew,* The People's Bible series (Milwaukee: Northwestern Publishing House, 1984), pp. 424-426.

31

Eternal peace was and is available to anyone who believes in Jesus as their Savior. But here's the irony: This peace also produces conflict.

Jesus said, "Do not suppose that I have come to bring peace to the earth. I did not come to bring peace, but a sword. For I have come to turn 'a man against his father, a daughter against her mother, a daughter-in-law against her mother-in-law—a man's enemies will be the members of his own household'" (Matthew 10:34-36).

Families are divided in belief. Neighbors, coworkers, and friends have different opinions about who Jesus was and is and what, if any, role he should play in our lives.

Therein is the struggle. Believing in Jesus as your Savior gives you eternal peace but very often also gives you temporal strife, as you are at odds with the unbelieving world. That discord is the Christian's lot as long as he or she is an inhabitant of earth. In heaven our peace will be complete. But as long as we are on earth, walking with Jesus will mean discord.

John quoted Jesus: "If the world hates you, keep in mind that it hated me first. If you belonged to the world, it would love you as its own. As it is, you do not belong to the world, but I have chosen you out of the world" (John 15:18,19).

Application/Discussion

8. In what ways has being a follower of Christ put you at odds with the rest of the world?

Believing in Jesus as your savior gives you eternal peace but very often also gives you temporal strife, as you are at odds with the unbelieving world.

9. In Jesus' prayer before he went to the Garden of Gethsemane, he prayed, "My prayer is not that you take them out of the world but that you protect them from the evil one. They are not of the world, even as I am not of it. Sanctify them by the truth; your word is truth" (John 17:15-17). What comfort is ours from this passage when we struggle with being at odds in the world?

Peace

Key takeaways

- The peace of God is not the worldly idea of peace. Rather, the peace of God is ours as a result of Jesus paying for our sins.

- Too often we go to war over things that don't really matter, or we lose sight of the fact that God controls everything.

- We can be tricked into settling into a peaceful setting that is not spiritually safe.

- At times, a separation has to occur for peace to happen. It shouldn't be a believer's first resort, but rather the course of action when other actions have failed.

- During times of separation, we can still pray for God to work mightily in hearts to restore the peace that momentarily seems unattainable.

- Very often the eternal peace we have is at war with those in the world who reject Jesus. This is a cross the believer bears until she reaches her heavenly home.

Prayer to close   Almighty God, we thank you for graciously bestowing your peace on every believer. Bless our efforts to touch others with the saving truth that Jesus is their salvation. Where strife exists because of our faith in you, help us to react to hatred with kindness and to react to insult with love. In this way may our lives be a pleasing offering to you and a bright light to a dark world. Jesus, we pray in your mighty name because of your precious blood. Amen.

Patience

Mollie Schairer

Definition: *The ability to accept delay, annoyance, or suffering without complaining or becoming angry; an active endurance of opposition*

Prayer to open Dear Holy Spirit, be with us and enlighten us as we learn patience from the apostle Paul. Show us how we have failed to be patient. Assure us of the complete forgiveness that our Savior earned for us. Strengthen us to be patient when others mistreat us and when we are in pain. In Jesus' name we pray. Amen.

Enduring patiently when others mistreat us

"Therefore, as God's chosen people, holy and dearly loved, clothe yourselves with . . . patience" (Colossians 3:12). In this passage and many others, the apostle Paul urged first-century believers to be patient. Sisters, bearing the fruit of patience is just as critical for us today. We need patience for the everyday trials: The five-year-old who refuses to eat anything that is not white; the aging parent who refuses to follow his doctor's recommended diet. And we need infinite patience with the woman ahead of us in line who asks to have her groceries rung up on two separate bills and then spends several minutes rooting around for coupons in her purse and on

Patience

her phone. (Please allow me to apologize right here for the times that I have been that woman!)

Yet showing patience as women of God encompasses much more. How do we live out patient endurance with those who mistreat us? How do we endure when we are in pain?

To help us be patient in these challenging circumstances, we look at the apostle Paul. He not only "talked the talk" in his preaching and teaching, but he also "walked the walk" throughout his difficult life. Paul poured his passion, energy, and talents into sharing the gospel. His message earned him enemies at nearly every stop in his missionary journeys. Many hated him: Gentiles and fellow Jews; influential, high-powered individuals; and common folks. He endured rejection, derision, unjust accusations, arrests, imprisonment, severe beatings, and mob violence, including an attempt to stone him to death. Yet he never returned violence for violence or hatred for hatred. Instead, he displayed a radical patience with his enemies.

Paul's patience with his enemies was marked by frequent prayer on their behalf. What was Paul's chief prayer for his persecutors? In Romans 10:1 he wrote of the fellow Jews who so often stirred up trouble for him: "Brothers and sisters, my heart's desire and prayer to God for the Israelites is that they may be saved."

Paul's patience with his enemies was marked by frequent prayer on their behalf.

During his trial before King Agrippa, Paul again expressed his desire for salvation for both Jews and Gentiles, including those who mistreated him. Paul, bound in chains, proclaimed, "Short time or long—I pray to God that not only you but all who are listening to me today may become what I am, except for these chains" (Acts 26:29). Paul, in his patient endurance of his enemies' hatred and violence against him, never stopped praying for them to come to faith and join him as brothers and sisters in Christ.

Do you have an enemy? Is there someone you avoid at all costs . . . or someone you wish you could avoid but cannot—someone who makes your life so much more difficult than it needs to be? Perhaps a former friend now gossips about you. Perhaps someone at work sabotages your work at every turn. Maybe you were in a relationship with someone who now seems bent on making you miserable. Perhaps you are suffering persecution from someone at work, at school, or in your own family, and their snide remarks or rejection hurt you. Maybe it is not you who is suffering mistreatment but your child or husband.

How do we respond? Maybe we refrain from doing physical harm to them, but we strike back by harming their reputation. Maybe outwardly we appear to endure patiently, but our heart's desire is for that person to be served up all the horrible things he or she deserves. Maybe we can't even imagine that such a person would come to faith, and therefore it would never occur to us to pray for his or her salvation.

We look again to the example of the apostle Paul. Why did he show such remarkable patience toward those who mistreated him? Simply because God had shown incredible patience toward *him*. Paul had been an enemy of God—his mission in life was to destroy all Christians! Paul, then called Saul, was on his way to Damascus to arrest all believers so they could be executed when Jesus appeared to him and changed his heart (Acts 9:1-19).

Paul patiently endured mistreatment, and he prayed fervently for his enemies to come to faith, because he never forgot who he was without Christ and how he became a part of God's family. He wrote to Timothy, "Here is a trustworthy saying that deserves full acceptance: Christ Jesus came into the world to save sinners—of whom I am the worst. But for that very reason I was shown mercy so that in me, the worst of sinners, Christ Jesus might display his immense patience as an example for those who would believe in him and receive eternal life" (1 Timothy 1:15,16).

The apostle Paul understood that it was purely God's undeserved mercy, expressed with seemingly unending patience toward him, that turned him around, forgave him completely, and made him part of God's family. And if God could do that for Paul, a violent, hate-filled persecutor of the church, God could do the same for those who mistreated him.

Sisters, God can do the same for those who cause us trouble. He has *already* done it for you and me! Most of us were not persecutors of the Church. But we too have an ugly past. We were enemies of God, just as Paul was (Colossians 1:21). God showed immense patience toward us. His Holy Spirit turned us around, forgave us completely, and made us part of his family. Every conversion is a miracle, dependent on God's loving patience toward us and totally independent of any contribution on our part. For both Paul and us, "the grace of our Lord was poured out on [us] abundantly" (1 Timothy 1:14)!

Application/Discussion

1. The King James Version often translated the Greek words for "patience" as "long-suffering." The 2011 New International Version

Patience

makes use of the word forbearance. Look up the meanings of *long-suffering* and *forbearance*. How do they contribute to your understanding of *patience*? Which of the three words is most meaningful for you?

2. Review some of the ways the apostle Paul was mistreated by reading Acts 14:19,20; Acts 16:22-24; and Acts 21:30-35. What do you think would have been hardest to endure patiently?

3. In thinking about someone who has mistreated you, why is it so difficult to respond with patience?

4. What would you pray for on behalf of a person who causes trouble for you, and what would you pray for on your own behalf?

God's power enables us to endure patiently when we are in pain

In his second letter to the Corinthians, the apostle Paul revealed a very personal pain: "I was given a thorn in my flesh, a messenger of Satan, to torment me. Three times I pleaded with the Lord to take it away from me" (2 Corinthians: 12:7,8).

We don't know exactly what this "thorn in [the] flesh" was. Many Bible commentators believe that it was some kind of chronic physical ailment. Some have speculated that the torment may have been mental. It certainly caused Paul a great deal of distress. He asked God repeatedly to take it away.

We've seen how the apostle Paul suffered at the hands of his enemies. Added to that trouble was an ailment that caused still more pain. Did he think, "Already I must endure so much, God, why can't you remove this thorn?" Or perhaps, "Lord, I could do even more in your service if I didn't have this painful condition weighing me down!"

We don't know the content of Paul's prayers or what was going through his mind. We know God's answer, though. He did not say, "Yes, Paul. Certainly, I will take it away. That only makes sense." Instead, God said, "My grace is sufficient for you, for my power is made perfect in weakness." Three times the Lord said, "No, my child. No."

And to God's repeated "no," we have Paul's response. He didn't question God's decision. He didn't kick and scream. He wrote, "Therefore, I will boast all the more gladly about my weaknesses, so that Christ's power may rest on me. That is why, for Christ's sake, I delight in weaknesses, in insults, in hardships, in persecutions, in difficulties. For when I am weak, then I am strong" (2 Corinthians 12:9,10).

The apostle Paul had his answer. He would need to endure patiently. And so he did. In his patient endurance of his condition, the Holy Spirit opened his eyes to an important truth. Paul was doing amazing things for the Lord, despite hatred, mistreatment, and violence at the hands of his enemies. Yet this thorn served as a constant and necessary reminder that he was doing it all through Christ's power, not his own.

Sisters, this truth is for us! We too possess *the very power of God working in us*. Let's turn to a portion of Paul's letter to the Colossians: "We continually ask God to fill you with the knowledge of his will through all the wisdom and understanding that the Spirit gives, so that you may live a life worthy of the Lord and please him in every way: bearing fruit in every good work, growing in the knowledge of God, being strengthened with all power according to his glorious might so that you may have great endurance and patience" (Colossians 1:9-11).

What does it mean to be "strengthened with all power according to [God's] glorious might"? A study guide on this section of Scripture proposes an alternate translation of this phrase. We are "mightily empowered with his glorious strength."[5]

Wow! You and I are mightily empowered with God's own limitless, glorious strength. This is the very power that created the world, that devised and carried out the plan of salvation, that raised Jesus from the dead, and that exalted him as ruler over the universe! Paul wrote to the Ephesians, "I pray

---

[5] Armin J. Panning, *Christ is All and in All: An Interactive Study of Colossians,* WELS Seminary Essay Files, p. 5

Patience

that the eyes of your heart may be enlightened in order that you may know... his incomparably great power for us who believe" (Ephesians 1:18,19).

It is my prayer too, sisters, that our eyes and hearts be opened by the Holy Spirit to understand what Paul understood, and the truth to which he clung in the midst of his pain. We have working in us a mighty power, a glorious supernatural strength. It is this strength, *God's* strength, that brought us to faith. Because of this faith, we are able to endure patiently the pain of chronic illness, the difficulties of aging, or any other thorn that God calls us to bear. For when we are weak, then we are strong.

> *We have working in us a mighty power, a glorious supernatural strength.*

Application/Discussion

5. Are you struggling with a thorn in your flesh? It may be a chronic physical or mental illness. Perhaps you are aging and developing painful, troublesome difficulties. Perhaps it is a "chronic" family problem that causes pain. Share your thorn as you feel comfortable.

6. What has your attitude been toward your thorn? How would it change if you were to consider it as something God was asking you to patiently endure for your sake and his glory?

7. At least in Scripture, Paul quickly moved from asking that the thorn be removed to accepting it as part of his life. Often it is not so easy. What things could help us to move from asking to accepting God's "no" or "not now"?

8. God's limitless, glorious power is at work in you. Too often our focus is on the thorn. What can we do to focus less on the thorn and more on God's power? What does it mean for you personally that God's limitless, glorious power is at work in *you*?

A life of perfect patience lived for me

All too often, we have not shown the fruit of patience in our lives. Our reflections on our attitudes toward our thorns, and how we have responded to those who mistreat us, bring us face-to-face with our failures. I know this to be true when I look honestly at my own life. I see reactions of anger and vengefulness toward those who have hurt me and resentful complaints when God calls me to bear some kind of hardship.

Let's turn to one last example of patience in the face of mistreatment and suffering. This time, we go to the cross. The Holy Spirit tells us through Luke, "Two other men, both criminals, were also led out with [Jesus] to be executed. When they came to the place called the Skull, they crucified him there, along with the criminals—one on his right, the other on his left. Jesus said, 'Father, forgive them, for they do not know what they are doing'"(Luke 23:32-34).

Jesus prayed for his executioners, the very soldiers pounding the nails into his hands! He didn't call down legions of angels to rescue and avenge him, though he had the power and the right. He refrained. He held back. He endured. And he asked his heavenly Father to forgive them.

In this prayer, we see Jesus' attitude of patient love toward those who sent him to an unjust death: Judas who betrayed him, the Jewish leaders who condemned him, the mob who hated him, and Pontius Pilate who failed him. Above all else, the desire of Jesus' heart was that they receive forgiveness and right standing with his Holy Father.[6]

The apostle Paul and Jesus both prayed for the salvation of those who hurt them. Both serve as examples to emulate. But Jesus' prayer means so much more. As he prayed, he gave up himself as the *answer.*

---

[6] For more on Jesus' prayer on the cross, see *The Theology of the Cross* by Daniel M. Deutschlander, pp. 261-266.

Patience

We too sent Jesus to an unjust death. Jesus prayed this prayer while suffering on the cross to pay for our sins of impatience, vengefulness, and complaining. Shortly after speaking these words, he would experience his Holy Father's total rejection, as God the Father punished him in our place. Jesus prayed for his Father to forgive his executioners, knowing that his own sacrificial death was the only way they—and we—could receive forgiveness from a just God.

Jesus' prayer assures us that he fulfilled every one of his Father's commands. Because we cannot keep God's law as he requires, Jesus was doing it for us, right up through his last agonizing moments. His lifetime of perfect patience, including this prayer of patient endurance, is now credited to us.

"Therefore, as God's chosen people, holy and dearly loved, clothe yourselves with . . . patience" (Colossians 3:12).

Sisters, we are God's chosen people. God showed his undeserved patience toward us in choosing us to be part of his family even though we were his enemies. We are dearly loved by a Savior who died to pay for our failures. God now sees us as holy, blameless, and spotless because Jesus' lifetime of perfect patience is ours through faith. With God's own glorious strength mightily at work in us, we are empowered to be patient, even through mistreatment and pain. Let us put on patience every day and wear it through every circumstance, thanking and glorifying our ever-patient God.

> *Jesus prayed for his Father to forgive his executioners, knowing that his own sacrificial death was the only way they—and we—could receive forgiveness from a just God.*

Application/Discussion

9. Where or with whom do you have a tendency to fail to be patient? Share your struggles as you feel comfortable. Whether or not you share them aloud, confess them to God.

10. How is Jesus' prayer on the cross an example to you when others mistreat you?

11. Jesus' prayer goes beyond an example to emulate. What does his prayer mean for you personally?

12. Discuss some strategies to aid you in the daily practice of putting on patience.

Key takeaways

- Follow the apostle Paul's example and pray that those who mistreat us grow in the grace and knowledge of the Lord Jesus.

- We can, like the apostle Paul, see our pain as a means of glorifying God, rather than a reason to complain.

- God's undeserved patience toward us motivates us to show patience toward others.

- God's own strength is at work in us, empowering us to be patient.

- On the cross, Jesus died to pay for our sins of impatience and finished his work of living out perfect patience in our place.

Prayer to close   Dear heavenly Father, we praise you for your limitless patience, which chose us to be your own beloved daughters. Dear Savior Jesus, we thank you for going to the cross to pay for our failures to be patient and for living the life of perfect patience that we could not. Dear Holy Spirit, encourage and empower us to be patient when we are mistreated and when we are in pain. It is your glory we seek, dear triune God. Amen.

Kindness

Mollie Schairer

Definition: *The quality of being generous, helpful, and caring about other people; an attribute of God*

Prayer to open   Dear Holy Lord, thank you for recording in Scripture the account of Ruth and Boaz. Help us learn from their example of kindness. Deepen our understanding of your loving kindness in caring for our bodies and in redeeming our souls. We humbly acknowledge that we have done nothing to deserve either. Enable us to shine more brightly in our unkind world, reflecting your kindness to our families and to everyone you have placed in our lives. Amen.

Learning kindness from a love story

Has kindness fallen by the wayside in our callous, me-first culture? Crude name-calling among our leaders and hurtful comments online make us cringe. We ourselves get caught up in a frantic busyness that blinds us to the needs of others. If there were such a thing as a "kindness meter," how would you rate our world? Your community? Your family? Yourself?

There was another time in history when the reading on the "kindness meter" was truly dismal. This bleak situation was among God's own chosen people. He had given them the Law of Moses so that their society could shine before all nations in bright reflection of God's kindness to them. Instead, they broke all the rules, took advantage of each other, ignored the needy, and lived for themselves. This was the time of the judges, when "everyone did as they saw fit" (Judges 21:25).

During this loveless, unkind era, Scripture records an unexpected love story of selfless kindness. Open your Bible and read Ruth chapters 1 and 2.

Ruth gives us a beautiful example of self-sacrificing kindness within families. In choosing to accompany Naomi to Bethlehem, she made a lifelong commitment to her mother-in-law, no matter the personal cost. It was very unlikely that Ruth, a foreigner, would find a husband in Bethlehem. At this time in history, marriage was a woman's only means of support. Ruth agreed to leave her family and her country, likely headed for a life of destitution in a strange land. Yet she pledged that she would never leave Naomi's side.[7]

When Ruth and Naomi arrived in Bethlehem, Ruth showed further kindness. She was willing to do whatever was needed to provide for Naomi, and to do so graciously. She offered to glean—pick up leftover grain—for them both. Her offer was practical, as she was younger and probably more physically able. It also showed kind sensitivity to Naomi's feelings. Ruth knew how humiliating it would have been for Naomi to glean the fields of old friends in her hometown.

God also calls us to bear the fruit of kindness within our own families. Though we may not have to give up all that Ruth freely relinquished, every kindness does require a sacrifice. We sacrifice our time as we nurture our children, serve our husbands, or care for elderly parents. We sacrifice our preferences as we accommodate family members. We sacrifice our pride as we end an argument with a kind word and an admission of our own wrongdoing, rather than seek an apology for the wrong done to us.

Do we, like Ruth, accept the cost of kindness with a gracious spirit? Do we lend a kind hand or a kind ear with sensitivity and tact? Do we consent to the rearrangement of our schedule that comes with performing an act of kindness? Do we mentally erase the "scoreboard" so that there is no tally of wrongs committed against us, or tally of kindnesses for which our family members owe us? Sisters, let's strive for a kindness that never resents the sacrifice or counts the cost. Let us practice a kindness that lovingly protects

---

[7] For more on Ruth's pledge, see *Judges, Ruth,* from The People's Bible series, by Dr. John C. Lawrenz, pp. 225-227; and *Ruth: Living in God's Unfailing Faithfulness,* by Naomi Schmidt, pp. 56-69.

Kindness

the feelings of others, especially those closest to us, the family God has given us. In doing so, we live out the loving kindness that the apostle Paul describes: "Love is patient, love is kind. . . . It does not dishonor others, it is not self-seeking, it is not easily angered, it keeps no record of wrongs" (1 Corinthians 13:4,5).

For his part, Boaz is an excellent example for us, showing how we might demonstrate kindness to those God puts in our paths. His words and actions went beyond the requirements of the law and the cultural expectations of the day. He noticed Ruth in his fields and approached her right away to extend generous kindness. He ensured that she had water while work-

Sisters, let's strive for a kindness that never resents the sacrifice or counts the cost.

ing. He invited her to eat with his workers, though there was no requirement in the Law of Moses to provide meals for those who gleaned, nor was it the Israelite custom. Boaz told his men to protect her, no small kindness toward this vulnerable immigrant woman. He also instructed them to leave behind extra grain on purpose, again going beyond what God had commanded in the Law of Moses.

Boaz showed yet another unexpected kindness when he spoke a biblical blessing to Ruth: "May the LORD repay you for what you have done. May you be richly rewarded by the LORD, the God of Israel, under whose wings you have come to take refuge" (2:12). Boaz acknowledged this foreign immigrant as a fellow God-follower and asked the Lord to protect her and richly bless her. His words of comfort and encouragement deeply touched Ruth.

We don't need to look far for people in need of our kind words and gestures. We need only, like Boaz, to keep our eyes open. Boaz was a wealthy man with much to manage during the busy harvest season. It would have been easy for him to overlook Ruth. He would have had excuses to do so. We too have our excuses for failing to notice the needs around us.

People in our communities need what Ruth and Naomi needed: food, safety, and a means of support. People in our church need to feel they belong. There are people at work, at school, at the gym, and *anywhere* we go who just need to know someone cares.

Noticing the need is only the first step. Kindness is love *in action*. Boaz acted as soon as possible, despite a busy schedule. His kindness reached above and beyond what might have been expected. He wasn't content with doing the minimum. Let's seek to do the same for the people God puts in our paths. And let us never forget the power of a kind word, especially one drawn from the promises of Scripture.

Application/Discussion

1. Think of a time that someone showed you kindness that touched your heart. What did it teach you about kindness?

2. List the ways that Boaz showed kindness to Ruth. What do his words of blessing (Ruth 2:12) reveal about his motivation?

3. What are the challenges in showing kindness to our family members?

> *Despite our ungrateful attitudes, God in his undeserved kindness continues to provide abundantly.*

4. The story of Ruth and Boaz illustrates for us that no encounter is chance, but rather God puts people in our paths. How does knowing this aid you in showing kindness to coworkers, classmates, neighbors, and church members?

A kind God behind the story

In arranging for Ruth to glean in Boaz's field, and working the fruit of kindness in Boaz's heart, God provided abundantly for Ruth and Naomi's bodily needs. Sisters, he does the same for us. We go to the grocery store and see row upon row of food. And we don't just look at it longingly; we have the means to select even more than we need, pay for it, and load it into our cars. The simple act of grocery shopping witnesses to the marvel

Kindness

of God's kind provision. We rarely think of it that way. In fact, during *my* last shopping trip, my sinful old Eve complained about the difficulties of shopping with little ones, the slow checkouts, and my realization that our favorite orange juice was now being sold in a smaller container for the same price. Sound familiar? Despite our ungrateful attitudes, God, expressing undeserved kindness, continues to provide abundantly.

God's abundant provision for Naomi and Ruth went beyond satisfying their immediate physical needs upon their return to Bethlehem. He had much, much more in store for them—and for Boaz.

In chapter 3 of the Bible account, we learn that Ruth made Boaz a humble proposal of marriage at the end of the harvest season. Included in this proposal was a request that Boaz buy back the ancestral land once belonging to Naomi's deceased husband, which they apparently had needed to sell some time before.[8] Ruth, following Naomi's instructions, went to the threshing floor one night. There she found Boaz, uncovered his feet, and lay down. When Boaz awoke, Ruth made her proposal. In the original Hebrew, she said, "Spread your wings over your servant girl." The Hebrew word for "wings" also meant the corner of a man's outer garment, with which he would cover himself at night. With these words, Ruth made her request for Boaz to take her as his wife, while reminding Boaz of the blessing he spoke to her the day they met. [9]

What was Boaz's response? "The Lord bless you, my daughter. . . . I will do for you all you ask" (Ruth 3:10,11). In a formal legal proceeding, Boaz affirmed his purchase of Naomi's deceased husband's ancestral land. In doing so, he assumed the role of "kinsman redeemer," a relative of means who willingly redeems, or buys back, family land. He also publicly proclaimed that Ruth would be his wife. And the joyful result of their marriage? "Boaz took Ruth and she became his wife. When he made love to her, the Lord enabled her to conceive, and she gave birth to a son" (Ruth 4:13).

God was keenly aware of Ruth and Naomi's needs when the two bereaved, destitute women made their way to Bethlehem. Though their story began

---

[8] Ehimelech, Naomi's husband, may have sold the right to farm the land, rather than the land itself. If this is the case, it did not change the situation of Naomi's destitution and the need for her to have a relative of means buy back the land. Unlike today's common practice of renting one's land to a farmer for cash payments or a portion of the crops each season, the Israelite practice of selling harvest rights meant that the seller would *not* receive any ongoing economic benefit from the land. For more on selling harvest rights, including the reason behind this practice, see *Ruth: Living in God's Unfailing Faithfulness*, p. 141.

[9] See *Judges, Ruth*, from The People's Bible series, by Dr. John C. Lawrenz, p. 246.

with tragedy, God had a plan to bless them beyond their imagining. The once desolate Naomi now had a new family: Ruth, her son-in-law Boaz, and a precious grandson. She also had the security of having her deceased husband's ancestral land restored to her, land that would remain in the family. Ruth was blessed with an amazing change in status. She went from impoverished foreigner to beloved wife and mother of high standing in the community. Boaz gained a selfless, God-fearing wife—and a son.

As we contemplate God's rich kindness to Naomi, Ruth, and Boaz, we can't help but reflect on the many kindnesses God has shown *us*. Consider the blessings in your life. These gifts may include a godly spouse, children, your job or means of income, good health, a rich heritage of faith, a family that loves you, and a church family that loves you.

We are reminded again and again that God knows our needs, meets those needs, and lavishes us with still more. His kind provision of our needs is what motivates us to meet the needs of those around us through our own kind actions. In doing so, we, like Ruth and Boaz, shine in bright reflection of *his* kindness.

Application/Discussion

5. Think about a time when you had a need and God answered your prayer in unexpected ways. Did his kind provision for you go above and beyond what you hoped? Share your answered prayer as you feel comfortable.

6. Recap the blessings that Naomi, Ruth, and Boaz received. With whom do you identify most?

7. Read Psalm 145:15-17 and Acts 14:17. What do these passages teach you about the Lord's kindness?

8. How does knowing that the Lord's kindness is undeserved help you in showing kindness to others?

9. How does knowing that God takes charge of meeting your needs help you in meeting the needs of others?

Jesus and us: The greatest love story

Maybe you are going through the kind of season Naomi and Ruth experienced at the beginning of the book of Ruth. Maybe loved ones have left you. Perhaps you feel you don't belong anywhere. Maybe you are hurting right now, and God's kindness seems far from your life.

Or you might be carrying a load of guilt for the ways you have not been kind: angry words or a sarcastic tone toward family members, missed opportunities toward those God placed in your path, or unkind attitudes of resentment and "score-keeping" even while performing acts of kindness. Maybe, at the end of the day, you feel that God's kindness is for "holier" people like Ruth and Boaz, not for you.

Sisters, there is more to the story! The book of Ruth concludes with a genealogy (4:17-22). In reading this genealogy, we learn that Obed, the son born to Boaz and Naomi, is an ancestor of King David.[10] And King David, we know, is an ancestor of Jesus.

Yes, God had a plan to lavish Naomi, Ruth, and Boaz with great kindness; to give them each other; bless them with a baby boy; and ensure their lifelong security. But all the while, God was guiding their lives to bring to fruition a much bigger plan, one he had determined to carry out even before he created the world: the birth of their Savior, and ours.

It is this Savior who claims *us* in a love story much greater and more beautiful than even Boaz and Ruth's. This love story also began with tragedy.

---

[10] This genealogy does not list all generations. See *Judges, Ruth,* from The People's Bible series, by Dr. John C. Lawrenz, pp. 217-218.

In God's Orchard

Our first parents turned their backs on their Creator, though he had given them everything. Our oneness with God was broken. All of us came into this world spiritually destitute and desperate, with no way to restore our relationship with God.

Our Savior saw that there was no one else to rescue us. He stepped in as our kinsman-redeemer, paying the highest price to buy back not land, but our souls. He willingly consented to become one of us, to be mocked and mistreated for his perfect kindness, and to be cut off completely from his Father's loving kindness on the cross.

When we're hurting in this unkind world, and when we're ashamed of our failures, our Savior spreads his cloak over us, covering our sin with his own righteousness. He has changed our status from destitute outsider to his own radiant, beloved bride! As a husband readies a new home for his bride, so Jesus is preparing a beautiful home for us in heaven. In him we have total security; his rock-solid commitment to us will endure for eternity.

Our Savior calls us with words of love that we need to hear again and again: "I have loved you with an everlasting love; I have drawn you with unfailing kindness" (Jeremiah 31:3). "I spread the corner of my garment over you and covered your naked body. I gave you my solemn oath . . . and you became mine" (Ezekiel 16:8). "Do not be afraid; you will not be put to shame. . . . For your Maker is your husband—the LORD Almighty is his name" (Isaiah 54:4,5). "My Father's house has many rooms; if that were not so, would I have told you that I am going there to prepare a place for you? And if I go and prepare a place for you, I will come back and take you to be with me that you also may be where I am" (John 14:2,3).

> *When we're hurting in this unkind world, and when we're ashamed of our failures, our Savior spreads his cloak over us, covering our sin with his own righteousness.*

Sisters, these words of love are for each one of us! His willing sacrifice paid for all our sins of unkindness. They are swept away as certainly as the morning mist vanishes in the sun. Free from fear, we can trust our heavenly Husband to see us through any and every hard season. We look forward to the day when the hero of our love story will come, take us by the hand, and lead us out of this unkind world to our true home with him.

Until then, we strive to reflect God's undeserved kindness to everyone he has placed in our lives. We meet their needs through selfless actions and kind words. We take every opportunity to show them the greatest kindness:

Kindness

sharing a love story that Christ intended for them, too. "I will tell of the kindnesses of the Lord, the deeds for which he is to be praised, according to all the Lord has done for us" (Isaiah 63:7).

Application/Discussion

10. In what ways is Boaz like Jesus? In what ways are we like Ruth? How do these parallels help you to understand and appreciate more fully Jesus' kindness toward you?

11. Which Bible passage of God's love in this section is most meaningful for you? Why?

12. How does the passage you chose relate to your efforts to show kindness?

13. What is the greatest kindness we can show others? What are some concrete ways you can extend this kindness to the people in your life?

In God's Orchard

Key takeaways

- The love story of Ruth and Boaz gives us shining examples of selfless kindness.

- In *our* love story, our Redeemer stepped in to buy us back from sin and death and to make us his own forever.

- Because of God's undeserved kindness toward us, we strive to reflect his kindness to our families and to everyone whom God puts in our path.

Prayer to close   Dear Lord, we thank you for this opportunity to study kindness in the account of Ruth and Boaz. We confess to you our failures to show kindness. We rejoice in your complete forgiveness and our new status as your beloved bride. Bless our efforts to be kind to our families and everyone you place in our lives. Help us to view meeting their needs not as obligations but rather as gracious opportunities to reflect your kindness to us. Amen.

Goodness

Ann M. Ponath and Amber Albee Swenson

Definition: *The quality or state of being good, the opposite of evil*[11]

Prayer to open   Dear Lord, when I think of goodness, I think of you, especially in my salvation through Jesus! Thank you! Goodness is such a basic concept, but being good is so complex for me, a poor, miserable sinner. Please bless my study of this spiritual fruit. Help me see the true blessing of goodness in my life and in my heart. Help me in the daily struggle to be good. Forgive me for all the times I am anything but good. In Jesus, my Savior, I pray. Amen.

God Is Good

"Taste and see that the Lord is good; blessed is the man who takes refuge in him" (Psalm 34:8).

"Oh, my goodness!" The words *goodness* and *good* are constantly in our conversations. We wish "good morning" and "good night" to family, friends, coworkers, and total strangers. We label everything from children

---

[11] *Merriam Webster* online dictionary: https://www.merriam-webster.com/dictionary/goodness, accessed January 2019.

to pets and everything in between—work, weekends, books, movies, cars, concerts, games, choices, and neighbors—as "good."

While each individual's concept of what is good—especially when talking about food or music—may differ, God is good from eternity. The true definition of goodness on this earth goes all the way back to the beginning. The beautiful garden God created for Adam and Eve came with strict instructions, recorded in Genesis 2:16,17: "The LORD God commanded the man, 'You are free to eat from any tree in the garden; but you must not eat from the tree of the knowledge of good and evil, for when you eat from it you will certainly die.'" Then, just one chapter later, we read that the devil craftily led Eve to question God's goodness and love, citing the desirable God-like quality of "knowing good and evil" as reason enough to choose evil over good and to take the fruit and eat, thus plunging all people into total depravity.

We might wonder why a good God would allow this to happen. The People's Bible commentary on Genesis explains it this way:

> God never designed humans to be puppets or robots whom he regulates by pulling strings or pressing buttons. By placing the tree of the knowledge of good and evil in the garden God was giving Adam the opportunity of his own free will to obey God. In so doing God realized the risk involved, that Adam might choose to disobey him. When Adam came from the hand of his Creator, he was in a state of *created innocence*. By giving Adam the command not to eat, God was offering him the opportunity to progress from created innocence to *conscious holiness.* God wanted his highest creature to be holy by choice, not just by accident.[12]

Although the devil, the world, and our own sinful flesh continue to tempt us to doubt God, scriptural accounts covering thousands of years of the history of God's people clearly display his goodness. The Psalms explode with reminders! Psalm 136:1 testifies that God is good because his love is inexhaustible: "His love endures forever." In Psalm 103:2-4 we are reminded that God heals us physically and spiritually day by day: "Praise the LORD, my soul, and forget not all his benefits—who forgives all your sins and heals all your diseases, who redeems your life from the pit and crowns you with love and compassion." And Psalm 145:8,9 declares that God's goodness is for all people, even those who refuse to follow him: "The LORD is gracious

---

[12] John Jeske, *Genesis,* The People's Bible series (Milwaukee: Northwestern Publishing House, 1984), pp. 38-39.

Goodness

and compassionate, slow to anger and rich in love. The Lord is good to all; he has compassion on all he has made."

But it isn't just the psalms! Look at God's goodness in the account of Abraham and Abimelek. When Abraham came to a new territory, he feared that the men of the land might kill him to confiscate his wife Sarah because she was beautiful. So Abraham lied and said Sarah was his sister. Abimelek took Sarah, but before he had a chance to touch her, God appeared to Abimelek in a vision at night, demanding his life on account of Sarah. Abimelek reasoned with the Lord, pleading that he hadn't known that Sarah was a married woman. The next day Abimelek gave Sarah back to Abraham, untouched, thanks to God's mighty hand working for Sarah's good (Genesis 20).

And consider God's goodness in providing for his children in the desert. "The Lord says, 'During the forty years that I led you through the wilderness, your clothes did not wear out, nor did the sandals on your feet" (Deuteronomy 29:5). Even though their disobedience and stubborn refusal to trust God brought them to the desert, God preserved and provided for his people in miraculous ways, not just with shoes and clothes but with food and water too.

God delivered Hezekiah and the people of Israel from the Assyrians, and Esther and the Jews from Haman's evil plot. Even God's chastisements were meant for eternal good—to turn the people from evil to repentance.

How often haven't we seen God's goodness in the way he has mightily protected us? Hasn't he kept us safe in a storm or traffic or shielded us from the danger someone may have intended for us? Hasn't God in his goodness provided for us? He supplies not just our daily bread, he goes extravagantly above and beyond. And doesn't God still use circumstances to bring us back to him? He preserves and delivers us from those who would destroy us, sometimes without our even realizing what he has done.

Because of God's good and gracious hand, we are a people familiar with blessings. All people, not just believers, have access to God's goodness. "He causes his sun to rise on the evil and the good, and sends rain on the righteous and the unrighteous" (Matthew 5:45).

Application/Discussion

1. James 1:17 tells us, "Every good and perfect gift is from above, coming down from the Father of the heavenly lights, who does not change like shifting shadows." Make a list of the blessings—physical

and spiritual, big and small—that God, in his goodness, has placed in your life.

Because of God's good and gracious hand, we are a people familiar with blessings.

2. So often we forget God's eternal goodness, especially in the face of our natural evil. We blame him for our problems instead of blaming the fall into sin and life in a sinful world. Think of a time or times when God was working for good in the midst of a bad situation.

3. Sometimes God does not deliver us from persecution. In some parts of the world, believers are routinely killed for their faith. How is God's goodness to his people evident even in those circumstances?

God's people are called to goodness

For this reason, since the day we have heard about you, we have not stopped praying for you. We continually ask God to fill you with the knowledge of his will through all the wisdom and understanding that the Spirit gives, so that you may live a life worthy of the Lord and please him in every way: bearing fruit in every good work, growing in the knowledge of God. (Colossians 1:9,10)

Goodness

Abel, Abraham, Noah, Joseph, Moses, Hezekiah, Job, Mary, Tabitha, Peter—the Bible is full of examples of believers living out their faith. And how about Tychicus? That's one name that probably didn't spring to mind! Tychicus is mentioned only three times in the Bible, yet he played an important part in Paul's ministry. He accompanied him on at least one missionary journey and served as a messenger, delivering Paul's letters to the Colossians and to Philemon—letters that would become books of the Bible!

> Tychicus will tell you all the news about me. He is a dear brother, a faithful minister and fellow servant in the Lord. I am sending him to you for the express purpose that you may know about our circumstances and that he may encourage your hearts. He is coming with Onesimus, our faithful and dear brother, who is one of you. They will tell you everything that is happening here. (Colossians 4:7-9)

Paul's letters are full of names of people who were doing good. (See Romans 16:1-16 for a great example of this.) Paul told of fellow kingdom workers who supported ministry in important ways, helping the gospel spread worldwide for the first time!

We too can take Paul's advice to the Colossians and live a life worthy of the Lord, bearing the fruit of goodness. We do this as we teach Sunday school or lead Bible studies, when we help with vacation Bible school or visit the elderly, when we pray for our pastor or make a meal for the sick.

These are small things that on their own would not be considered great. So what makes good works good?

The apostle Paul tells us in Ephesians 2:8-10, "It is by grace you have been saved, through faith—and this is not from yourselves, it is the gift of God—not by works, so that no one can boast. For we are God's handiwork, created in Christ Jesus to do good works, which God prepared in advance for us to do."

Our good works are a result of faith—faith received as a gift. Since God is good, when we receive the Spirit through faith in Jesus, we are infused with the goodness of God. With this faith and the traits and abilities God gave us even before we were born, good works naturally pour out of us in service to God and others.

Our good works do not earn us special favor with God and shouldn't be done for the attention and admiration of men. Rather, they are a means of pointing the world to God. Jesus said, "When you give to the needy, do not announce it with trumpets, as the hypocrites do in the synagogues and on the streets, to be honored by others" (Matthew 6:2). Instead, we are to "let [our] light shine before others, that they may see [our] good deeds and glorify [our] Father in heaven" (Matthew 5:16).

And what qualifies as an act of goodness? Jesus mentioned giving to the needy. Tychicus delivered Paul's letter and encouraged the saints. In Romans chapter 16 Paul speaks of his benefactor, of those who opened their homes to him, those who stood by him, and those who were imprisoned with him. He mentioned a woman who mothered him and other women who worked hard with him. He spoke of those who befriended him. Jesus viewed even giving a cup of cold water to a child is an act worthy of commendation (Matthew 10:42).

Anything done in faith out of love for God and/or his people is a good work and is evidence of the Spirit living in us.

Application/Discussion

4. Think of a person in the Bible or in your life who is a Christian example of goodness. How has God blessed you through them?

Anything done in faith out of love for God and/ or his people is a good work and is evidence of the Spirit living in us.

5. Read Romans 16:1-16. Which acts of service mentioned by Paul are things you had never thought of? With these things in mind, what things could you do to serve God's people?

6. Genesis 6:5 and Psalm 51:5 assure us that our natural inclination is not toward goodness. Our selfishness will see works of service we could do but will decide against them. What must we do to combat our tendency toward evil and to instead be an ambassador of good?

Why goodness?

"You were once darkness, but now you are light in the Lord. Live as children of light (for the fruit of the light consists in all goodness, righteousness and truth) and find out what pleases the Lord" (Ephesians 5:8-10).

Evil is all around us in this sinful world. Evil is in us. Since the fall into sin, every tiny human baby is infected with it and there is no earthly cure. And not only are we born with sin, but we continuously choose evil over good. Psalm 14:2,3 is very clear: "The Lord looks down from heaven on all mankind to see if there are any who understand, any who seek God. All have turned away, all have become corrupt; there is no one who does good, not even one."

Paul, by inspiration, explains the quandary the sinner/saint experiences in Romans 7:18-20: "I know that good itself does not dwell in me, that is, in my sinful nature. For I have the desire to do what is good, but I cannot carry it out. For I do not do the good I want to do, but the evil I do not want to do—this I keep on doing. Now if I do what I do not want to do, it is no longer I who do it, but it is sin living in me that does it."

Dishonoring God and his Word, lying, cheating, stealing, selfish pride, unfaithfulness to our marriages, murdering in our thoughts, coveting our neighbors' goods—when we compare our actions and thoughts to God's commandments, we can see we are far, far from the absolute perfection he demands. Isaiah 64:6 tells us that even "our righteous acts are like filthy rags." How can we be good or even hope to do good if no goodness exists inside of us? We are entirely doomed.

In God's Orchard

Remember what resulted when Adam and Eve questioned God's goodness? Paul lays out the cold hard facts in Ephesians 2:1-5:

> As for you, you were dead in your transgressions and sins, in which you used to live when you followed the ways of this world and of the ruler of the kingdom of the air, the spirit who is now at work in those who are disobedient. All of us also lived among them at one time, gratifying the cravings of our flesh and following its desires and thoughts. Like the rest, we were by nature deserving of wrath. But because of his great love for us, God, who is rich in mercy, made us alive with Christ even when we were dead in transgressions—it is by grace you have been saved.

The ultimate example of goodness is our Savior—true God becoming true Man, born in the lowliest of situations, for us. Jesus not only perfectly fulfilled the Law in our place, but Scripture overflows with accounts of his goodness—wine for a wedding, healing for the sick, sight for the blind, food for five thousand, life for the dead! And then he set his face resolutely for Jerusalem (Luke 9:51) where he knew he'd endure horrific suffering and a brutal death, an innocent victim of our willful evil, in order to save us.

The ultimate example of goodness is our Savior—true God becoming true Man, born in the lowliest of situations, for us.

God loves us, wanted us; God chose us and was willing to pay the ultimate price to spend eternity with us. God said through Zephaniah that he takes great delight in us (Zephaniah 3:17). Those weren't just empty words. No, those were words he backed up with action to prove it—the sacrificing of his one and only Son to save us.

"So like the people in Luke 3, we ask, 'What then shall we do?' Not in the sense of 'What do I have to do to get this wrathful God off my back?' but rather in the sense of 'What can I do to thank my outrageously merciful Father for this undeserved joy of salvation he has so richly poured into my life?'"[13]

Quite simply, our fruits, such as goodness, show our Spirit-worked faith and our thankfulness for all that God in Christ has done! Remembering God's eternal goodness and thanking him for his rich blessings in Jesus, may we dedicate ourselves and our lives to his glory! Let's make the words of Hebrews 13:20,21 be our prayer. "May the God of peace, who through

---

[13] This paragraph was taken from a sermon given on December 9, 2018 by Pastor Michael Koepke.

Goodness

the blood of the eternal covenant brought back from the dead our Lord Jesus, that great Shepherd of the sheep, equip you with everything good for doing his will, and may he work in us what is pleasing to him, through Jesus Christ, to whom be glory forever and ever. Amen."

Application/Discussion

Remember Tychicus? Read the words he delivered from Paul to Philemon: "I pray that your partnership with us in the faith may be effective in deepening your understanding of every good thing we share for the sake of Christ. Your love has given me great joy and encouragement, because you, brother, have refreshed the hearts of the Lord's people" (Philemon 6,7).

7. What is the greatest good work we could do? How well do you do that?

8. Second Corinthians 9:8 says, "God is able to bless you abundantly, so that in all things at all times, having all that you need, you will abound in every good work." How does this combat the excuses we come up with for not being able to do good works?

9. Hebrews 10:24,25 advises: "Let us consider how we may spur one another on toward love and good deeds, not giving up meeting together, as some are in the habit of doing, but encouraging one another—and all the more as you see the Day approaching." What can you do to spur others on to good deeds?

In God's Orchard

Key takeaways

- True goodness begins with God. From eternity, God is and does only good.

- Spirit-worked faith produces fruits in believers' lives and blesses others.

- Because of our entirely sinful state, it is impossible to please God without faith.

- God's ultimate goodness was displayed in salvation through Christ.

- Jesus, our Savior, is a complete example of goodness. His perfect life and death cover our imperfections.

- Goodness and good works are reflections of faith, they demonstrate our thankfulness to God for his goodness, they bless and encourage others, and they glorify God!

Prayer to close   Heavenly Father, Thank you for sharing your goodness with us through your creation and the gifts you bestow on us. Thank you, Jesus, for being the goodness we could not be and showing the world what goodness is. Thank you, Holy Spirit, for bringing us to faith and putting your goodness in us. Continue to open our eyes to ways we can point the world to you. Forgive us for failing at this so often. Through the powerful name of our Savior, Jesus, we pray, Amen.

Faithfulness

Naomi Schmidt

Definition: *Unwavering, unfailing commitment*

Prayer to open   Heavenly Father, we gather around your Word to seek you. We come to learn more about your grace—and we find it here poured out in rich measure again and again through our Savior, Jesus Christ. In your Word, you faithfully keep your promises, offer forgiveness, and cover us with perfect righteousness. We lift our hearts to you in thanksgiving and love, trusting your grace and mercy. Teach us about you and strengthen your Spirit in our hearts through the Word. Transform our thoughts, words, and actions so that we may live for your glory with renewed zeal. Amen.

Meet our faithful God

In a broken world where hearts are overwhelmed with the pain of disappointment or shattered relationships, people scoff at the word *faithfulness*. Who is faithful? Who lives with unwavering commitment?

> The Word of God tells us faithfulness is the Lord's very essence.

In God's Orchard

Who is unfailing in their faithfulness? It seems at times we don't know anyone who is dependable. We long for someone who always keeps their promises, while the unbelieving world doesn't even know if such a thing exists.

In Scripture God shows us what unfailing faithfulness is—he shows us himself. God proves that since the beginning of time he has kept every promise and is perfectly committed to the salvation of his people. A word like *faithfulness* might describe the actions of some people some of the time, but the Word of God tells us faithfulness is the Lord's very essence. His being and character are the embodiment of faithfulness. He cannot be anything but faithful! Deuteronomy 7:9 says, "Know therefore that the Lord your God is God; he is the faithful God, keeping his covenant of love to a thousand generations of those who love him and keep his commandments." Jeremiah tells us: "The steadfast love of the Lord never ceases; his mercies never come to an end; they are new every morning; great is your faithfulness" (Lamentations 3:22,23 ESV).

There is tremendous comfort and great joy in the unfailing faithfulness of God. And because he gives us his Spirit and dwells within us, his faithfulness is ours.

But Scripture also shows us the reality of humanity's failure to be faithful. God puts sin on open display to make sure we never forget our need for a Savior. We see the unfaithfulness of Noah, drunken and exposed after God's demonstration of power and mercy (Genesis 9:20-27). We meet Zechariah, a high priest who hesitated to believe that God could bless him with a son in his old age (Luke 1:5-25). Then we read about a rich, young ruler who could not be faithful—even in the presence of Jesus (Matthew 19:16-22; Mark 10:17-23; Luke 18:18-25).

We too experience heartache, pain, and failed expectations. A family member is drawn away by worldly living, a loved one betrays our trust, or an unethical coworker undermines the solidarity in our workplace. Even in our churches we are disappointed by other's actions—or failure to act. Then, as a fatal blow, we look in the mirror of the law and are slayed by our own unfaithfulness: we jealously covet the blessings of others, disregard God's name and Holy Word, or fail to love all people with our whole heart. We are ungrateful, irritated, prideful, and selfish. Still, "the Lord longs to be gracious to you; therefore he will rise up to show you compassion. . . . How gracious he will be when you cry for help! As soon as he hears, he will answer you" (Isaiah 30:18,19).

Faithfulness

Application/Discussion

1. In the words just prior to these verses from Isaiah, God laments that his people stubbornly refuse to turn to him for help. Describe a situation where you've ignored God while trying to solve a problem by yourself (and failed miserably before turning to the Lord).

2. Read the following passages about God's unfailing faithfulness. What application does each verse have for our faith walk?
   a. Deuteronomy 32:4

   b. Psalm 89:8

   c. 1 Corinthians 1:8,9

   d. 1 Corinthians 10:13

   e. 1 John 1:9

3. Pick a phrase from Isaiah 30:18-19 to write out and memorize.

God breathes faithfulness into humanity

While God's unfailing faithfulness is beyond the grasp of humanity, he gives us his Spirit and makes us faithful when we become his children. Scripture highlights many Spirit-filled believers living out God's faithfulness—even in hardship. One such account is tucked away in the rich pages of Old Testament history, where you'll find a man named Hosea. His deep, heart-wrenching story is rooted in God's demand that Hosea be a living example of the Lord's faithfulness—by marrying a prostitute named Gomer.

The setting of Hosea's life is not unlike our culture with social priorities and moral standards that openly conflict with God's commands. The idolatry forbidden in the Old Testament is brazenly present in our world, and even in the self-chosen priorities we pursue in our own lives. Whether it is a life centered in the pursuit of earthly pleasures, unwillingness to yield to Christ, or the excessive exaltation of our possessions, our choices testify to our unfaithfulness and condemn us in the eyes of God. "A spirit of prostitution is in their heart; they do not acknowledge the Lord" (Hosea 5:4).

> *The idolatry forbidden in the Old Testament is brazenly present in the self-chosen priorities we pursue in our own lives.*

In this setting, God unites Hosea with a prostitute in marriage as a clear display of God's perfect faithfulness and commitment to a bride who is unworthy and unfaithful. Hosea and Gomer's union is blessed with three children. Then Gomer leaves her husband and children, returning to her life of prostitution.

Hosea's life becomes a crucible of refinement. In the midst of Gomer's adultery, the Lord commands Hosea to buy Gomer back from her insidious lifestyle. "Love her as the Lord loves the Israelites, though they turn to other gods" (Hosea 3:1).

At a time when adulterers were stoned to death, it might seem surprising that Hosea even spared her life. But as a beautiful demonstration of God's faithfulness, Hosea forgave her and even paid the price to get her back—Hosea fully restored her in the relationship as his wife.

This faithful love to an undeserving sinner spotlights the character of God. He is faithful because of who he is—not because of who we are. Look with awe at this fruit of faithfulness that is ours through the Holy Spirit.

God calls us to live with words and actions that speak clearly of undeserved grace and faithfulness. We are vessels and diffusers of God's faithfulness—not just in marriage but in all our relationships; not just in our commitment to our church but to the urgency of spreading the gospel to all people; not just to the people we love but to those who break our hearts like a bride defiled in prostitution. This faithful life is marked by self-sacrifice and submission to the Lord—and motivated by the grace of Christ.

Application/Discussion

4. We are both Gomer and Hosea. The unfaithful "Gomer" of our sinful nature is called to repentance; our new nature is called to live a faithful, Spirit-filled life, like Hosea. Satan tempts us to think of ourselves either mostly as Gomer or Hosea. Either can have serious ramifications. How so?

5. Whom do you tend to identify with?

God shows us Jesus through Abraham's faithfulness

Although we see the Lord's faithfulness throughout Abraham's life, there is one event that captures the magnitude of God's perfect faithfulness. This picture of faithfulness also gives us a glimpse of God's plan for salvation in Christ.

In Genesis 15:5 the Lord promised Abraham that his descendants would be as countless as the stars, but he and Sarah had to wait many, many years before their son, Isaac, was born. Imagine Abraham's devastation and confusion when God told him, "Take your son, your only son, whom you love—Isaac—and go to the region of Moriah. Sacrifice him there as a burnt offering" (Genesis 22:2).

Yet, early the next morning Abraham set out with his son as God commanded, and after three days they reached Mount Moriah. Abraham faithfully built an altar and assured Isaac that God would provide a lamb for the sacrifice. But when the altar was complete, he bound his son Isaac and laid him on the wood. "He reached out his hand and took the knife to slay his son. But the angel of the Lᴏʀᴅ called out to him from heaven, 'Abraham! Abraham! . . . Do not lay a hand on the boy. . . . Do not do anything to him. Now I know that you fear God, because you have not withheld from me your son, your only son'" (Genesis 22:10-12). Abraham was faithful because the faithfulness of God drove the fear and uncertainty from his heart.

The account of Abraham's faithfulness was not written to teach us what we must do to be faithful. Through Abraham God shows us the extent of his love for us in Christ. He isn't asking us, "Do you love me *this much*? Will you do *anything* for me?" Rather, he is showing what he gave for our salvation! He is saying, "*I* love you this much! *I* will do this for you!" Abraham's life lesson gives us a glimpse of God's sacrifice for sinners.

Through Abraham God shows us the extent of his love for us in Christ.

This poignant account draws us to the cross. Jesus lived every moment of his life in perfect faithfulness to God. Whether speaking to hungry crowds on a hillside or a broken woman at a well, he poured out the Father's forgiveness. Filled with passion for God's holiness and truth, he drove out demons and turned tables in the synagogue. He obeyed government officials who had no respect or understanding of who he was. He honored the gift of life with his compassion, fully mindful of the spiritual, emotional, and physical needs of everyone he met. He cared for his mother and gave grace to a thief in the last hours of his suffering. Then, in a final act of faithfulness to us, he died to give us a robe of righteousness.

We can be faithful because Jesus dwells in us and he is faithful.

Application/Discussion

6. The psalmist encourages us, "Trust in the Lᴏʀᴅ and do good; Dwell in the land and cultivate faithfulness" (Psalm 37:3 NASB). What practical, everyday things can you do to cultivate faithfulness?

7. Where are your greatest challenges in being faithful?

Faithfulness

8. We often think of the word *faithfulness* in the context of marriage or stewardship. How has this study broadened your understanding of what faithfulness looks like in the life of a believer?

Key takeaways

- On our own we are utterly faithless.

- The faithfulness of God is unfailing, unchanging, and eternal.

- His Spirit lives in us through faith. God dwells within us so we can be assured that we have the gift of faithfulness. It is part of who God is, and it is who we are in Christ.

- Jesus' life was marked by unwavering faithfulness to his Father and to undeserving people.

- Through Christ, faithfulness will shape our commitment to others with a focused concern for the salvation of all people.

Prayer to close   Lord God, we see in Scripture your unfailing faithfulness through the ages. We marvel at the Spirit-filled believers who reflected your faithfulness so beautifully—even in great hardship. Fill us with a great measure of your Spirit that we may draw others to see you. Give us strength, courage and wisdom to be unwavering in our faithfulness and to boldly live for you. Open our eyes to see the lost, turn our ears to hear the lonely, and then unloose our tongues to speak of what Christ has done for sinners! All these things are for your glory alone. Amen.

Gentleness

Katie Martin

Definition: *Kind, amiable, free from harshness, willingness to yield, softness in action*[14]

Prayer to open   Dear Lord, teach me to practice gentleness. Fuel my pursuit of gentleness by your grace and love. Give me your Spirit to grow my faith and my ability to serve you in all things. In Jesus' name. Amen.

The pursuit of gentleness

My parents taught me how to drive using their 1989 Toyota Camry. The Camry was a relatively new car with automatic transmission. They made it clear from the beginning that if I ever expected to take a car out on my own, it wasn't going to be that one. Upon receiving my license, I would be relegated to drivivng the Dodge Colt hatchback with a manual transmission. Anxious to have my own set of wheels, I set out to learn how to drive stick. While learning, the phrase, "Don't pop the clutch!" was repeated consistently. The volume of the phrase depended on the level of whiplash my dad was receiving at the time. After plenty of botched attempts, I learned that driving a manual transmission involves gentleness. You need to gradually release the clutch while gently and simultaneously stepping on the gas. A smooth start from first gear could only be achieved with a perfect balance of release and pressure.

[14] Definitions taken from www.dictionary.com and www.biblestudytools.com, 2019.

Gentleness

In this chapter, we are going to explore the spiritual fruit of gentleness. While you might need gentleness or a light touch to drive a stick shift, the definition of gentleness for our Christian lives goes far beyond that. Gentleness doesn't imply weakness, spinelessness, or an unwillingness to act. Rather, gentleness implies that one acts but does so softly, with the best interest of others at heart.

Sounds easy enough, right? Well, not really. While gentleness is a fruit that all Christians possess through faith in Christ, it isn't a characteristic that comes to us naturally. If you have had your patience tried by an ignorant coworker, a critical unbeliever, or a strong-willed child, you know that gentleness can be difficult to put into practice. The apostle Paul alludes to the difficulty of putting on a spirit of gentleness in his letter to Timothy. "You, man of God, flee from all this, and pursue righteousness, godliness, faith, love, endurance and gentleness. Fight the good fight of the faith" (1 Timothy 6:11,12).

Before discussing the pursuit of gentleness, let's focus on the imperative that the Holy Spirit inspired Paul to give directly before he listed what Paul should pursue. *Flee.* Flee from all of "this." A look at the preceding verses (vs. 6-10) reveals that the "this" is the love of money. But the "this" can be any sinful desire that crowds out Jesus and vies for first place in our hearts. Following these sinful desires can push us away from Christ and plunge us into spiritual ruin. Any pursuit of the spiritual characteristics the Lord calls us to possess must begin with a flight from those selfish desires. We can only run towards the things God wants for us, as we run away from the things we want for ourselves. This isn't a natural tendency.

Now focus on Paul's second imperative—pursue. Pursuit isn't a lackadaisical walk towards a goal; rather, it implies a chase with obstacles in the way, like a harrowing car chase or a manhunt by the police.

What do you pursue? Do you pursue excellence at your job, earthly success, a good reputation, happiness? Admittedly, gentleness didn't make my list. Yet, the apostle Paul includes it on his list to denote its importance in the life of a Christian.

Teachers tell students to go with their first instinct when taking a test. Statistically, your first answer is more likely to be correct. The longer you take to deliberate an answer, the higher the margin for error. The opposite is true in our Christian faith walk. Our first thought is usually to gratify self instead of others. By nature, we want to be right, win an argument at all costs, and criticize those who challenge or annoy us. Flee from those first instincts and pursue gentleness.

In God's Orchard

King David engaged in adultery and premeditated murder. When he was confronted by the prophet Nathan, David repented and was given God's full forgiveness. As a consequence of his sin, Nathan told David that there would be calamity in his household (2 Samuel 12:11). Also, his infant son would die (2 Samuel 12:14). The description of David's family life in 2 Samuel chapters 13-18 reads like a soap opera. At the heart of most of this drama was his son Absalom. Absalom spread lies about his father to win the hearts of Israel and started a rebellion to steal the kingdom.

Imagine an immediate family member talking behind your back, spreading lies about you, and trying to take your property by force. My natural response would be anything but gentle. I would defend my reputation, even if it meant dragging someone else's name through the mud. I might even resort to force, anger, or revenge to get my property back.

This time David didn't fall into a trap laid by sinful desires. As his men attempted to deal with the rebellion, he had a very specific request for his men: "Be gentle with the young man Absalom for my sake" (2 Samuel 18:5). He put a spirit of gentleness on display before his entire army. Although he was going to act to restore himself as the rightful ruler of Israel, he had the soul of his son Absalom at heart. He wanted his son to repent of his sins and receive the free, full grace of God.

The pursuit of gentleness is a lifelong struggle between acting the way we want and the way God wants us to act. David's confidence in his complete forgiveness and his love for God gave him the power to walk the balance. It's no different for us. Only in view of his great mercy can we walk the path of righteousness and put on a spirit of gentleness.

The pursuit of gentleness is a lifelong struggle between acting the way we want and the way God wants us to act.

Application/Discussion

1. Fleeing from the things our sinful nature wants and pursuing the things God wants for us results in blessings. Think about a time in your life when you acted in a brash, heated manner. Write about it below.

Gentleness

2. How might this situation have ended differently if you had put on a spirit of gentleness?

3. Read Proverbs 15:1. What happens in a volatile situation when we use harsh words? What does gentleness breed in our personal relationships?

4. Go back to 1 Timothy chapter 6. Read verses 6-10. What can the love of money (or the love of anything before God) do to our faith?

5. List the things Paul tells us to pursue in verse 11. How can you pursue these spiritual characteristics in your daily life?

6. Reread 1 Timothy 6:12. What does Paul tell us about this pursuit?

The pursuit of gentleness is not what the world expects

In 2016, Queen Elizabeth celebrated her 90th birthday. The United Kingdom went all out for the royal celebration. Village shops had special window displays, flags were hung everywhere, and it seemed each town prepared its own celebration to honor the queen. A Burger King in London even changed the name on its sign to Burger Queen. And those were just the preparations. The celebration itself went even further. Throngs of people lined the streets from Buckingham Palace to the Royal Horse Guards. The parade route was decorated with flags, balloons, and flowers, and the parade itself included soldiers, music, horses, and a Royal Air Force flyover.

Such fanfare is exactly what you might expect for the birthday celebration of a royal monarch. Yet, Christ was born in a stable, placed in a manger, and visited by lowly shepherds. The only royal procession for our Savior would be when he made his way to Jerusalem to be betrayed, tortured, and killed.

Ponder that the Lord Almighty uses feeble human bodies to do his work. He doesn't blare trumpets from heaven or send a lightning bolt every time he wants to save a soul. He does that almighty work in a quiet, gentle way. He comes to us gently in water and changes a sinful heart to one of his own. In a bite of bread and a drink of wine, he gives us himself. To the unbelieving world these look valueless, but to the Christian these sacraments offer untold comfort and yield unmatched power.

We often think the Lord should work more powerfully among us. If only he would forcefully stop the evil in the world around us, or grab our unbelieving friend by the proverbial shoulders and give her a good shake, maybe then she would come to faith. But who are we to tell the Lord how to work? People are brought to faith with the simple, sweet words of the gospel message and the power of the Holy Spirit, whom we cannot see. Not only does he come to us gently through Word and sacrament, but he also treats us gently as he deals with our failings time and time again. He is our Good Shepherd, gently guiding us through life and redirecting us when we stray.

As subjects of Jesus' kingdom, we are called on to act in gentleness. Refer back to 1 Timothy 6:11,12. The word that Paul uses for gentleness in the Greek is similar to the word that Jesus uses in his Sermon on the Mount in Matthew chapter 5:5, "Blessed are the meek, for they will inherit the earth." Meekness and gentleness are such important characteristics in the life of a

Gentleness

Christian that Jesus draws attention to them here. This meekness is an outward sign of a deep faith in Jesus within. Through this faith in Jesus alone, the meek and gentle will overcome this world and be ushered into eternal glory in heaven.

> *As subjects of Jesus' kingdom, we are called on to act in gentleness.*

As we pursue gentleness, we learn to act contrary to the world. The world says to seek revenge and to assert ourselves and get what we deserve. But Jesus tells us that gentleness is far more effective as we forge personal relationships. And how are we to respond to the insults of unbelievers? "In your hearts revere Christ as Lord. Always be prepared to give an answer to everyone who asks you to give the reason for the hope that you have. But do this with gentleness and respect" (1 Peter 3:15). "Let your gentleness be evident to all. The Lord is near" (Philippians 4:5). "As God's chosen people, holy and dearly loved, clothe yourselves with compassion, kindness, humility, gentleness and patience" (Colossians 3:12). Gentleness, gentleness, and even more gentleness.

Gentleness is all too often lacking. I am not gentle when talking to my husband about how he loads the dishwasher or folds the laundry. I am critical, unkind, and bring up things that are better left unsaid. (He does the laundry and loads the dishwasher, but I still complain about it!) I am not gentle when I "encourage" my daughter to do her best on her math homework or when my son takes the shampoo out of my shower and fails to put it back or my daughter leaves the house without turning her light off . . . again.

I am too quickly irritated and sarcastic with the customer service representative who doesn't give me what I want. The drivers on the road (and my passengers) hear a barrage of self-righteousness as I shout at them to use the left lane for passing only. The fans sitting next to me at the soccer game hear my criticism of the refs and the other team. My competitive spirit and desire to win bulldoze anyone who disagrees with me.

Gentleness sounds easy, but is difficult to execute. Nevertheless, gentleness is a fruit of the Spirit that the Lord promises will be exhibited in the life of a Christian. How do we take hold of this fruit? Again, we refer back to the words of the apostle Paul. *Fight the good fight.* God's mercies are new every day. We repent for the times we have failed to be gentle and pray for his power to continue our pursuit of gentleness.

Consider the reformer Martin Luther's advice to his wife, Katie. She was very independent and often unafraid to share her strong opinions. Luther once told Katie to curb her volubility by saying the Lord's Prayer before opening her mouth.[15] While Luther may have meant this to tease his beloved wife, it's a good reminder for us to pray first, speak later. Unfortunately, these two are almost always reversed. I speak unkindly, rashly, and without thinking, then have to pick up the pieces I shattered by my lack of gentleness.

Although I often fail, gentleness is something I remember long after the situation is over. Growing up, I almost never heard my parents exchange harsh words. Now that I'm married, I admire the gentleness they modeled in their relationship with each other. A colleague who had been wrongfully terminated spoke gently to that boss. Gentleness is so unexpected, but has a lasting effect on others.

Every day is a new opportunity to put God's grace on display as I pursue gentleness. When I fail, I pray for strength to do better. And for those days when gentleness wins, to God be the glory.

Application/Discussion

7. Read 1 Kings 19:1-3, 9-18. Elijah's mind-set must have quickly changed from triumph and confidence to fear and defeat. What do you find most comforting about the way God comforted Elijah here?

8. Think of a time when God comforted you in a gentle whisper.

9. Think of a time when gentleness had unexpected consequences in your life. Talk about it with your group.

---

[15] Roland H. Bainton, *Women of the Reformation in Germany and Italy* (Minneapolis: Augsburg Fortress Press, 1971), p. 37.

Gentleness

10. Now think about how Jesus deals with us in unexpected ways.
Discuss how that fact is meaningful to you and gives you comfort.

God's pursuit of us

God saw us, loved us in spite of our sinfulness, and pursued us. We were dead, entangled in sin and powerless to avoid the eternal punishment our sins deserved. But what amazing grace! Jesus didn't give up on us. Rather, he left heaven and orchestrated our rescue from the kingdom of darkness with his almighty power. "He reached down from on high and took hold of me; he drew me out of deep waters. He rescued me from my powerful enemy, from my foes, who were too strong for me" (Psalm 18:16,17).

As Jesus carried out this amazing rescue, he displayed this perfect, gentle love throughout his ministry. Even more incredibly, he displayed unfathomable gentleness during his time of suffering and death on the cross. If anyone had a reason to seek revenge, it was Jesus. Sinful men spit on him and slapped him. The worldly leaders—who had received their power from him—sentenced him to die. The sins of the whole world were set upon his back, though he hadn't committed a single sin. Listen to Isaiah's description of our gentle, humble Savior: "He was oppressed and afflicted, yet he did not open his mouth; he was led like a lamb to the slaughter, and as a sheep before its shearers is silent, so he did not open his mouth" (Isaiah 53:7). Through unimaginable pain he asked his Father to forgive his tormentors. He asked his dear friend to care for his mother.

As we seek to glorify Jesus and spread his message of life to the broken world around us, we keep our eyes fixed on Jesus. It's all about Jesus. He makes our earthly pursuits possible by His grace alone. "Let us run with perseverance the race marked out for us, fixing our eyes on Jesus, the pioneer and perfecter of faith. For the joy set before him he endured the cross, scorning its shame, and sat down at the right hand of the throne of God" (Hebrews 12:1,2). You and I, my friend, are the joy set before Jesus. He saw us. He pursued us even though it meant enduring the cross and the scorn.

In God's Orchard

As we seek to glorify Jesus and spread his message of life with the broken world around us, we keep our eyes fixed on Jesus.

He continues to display gentleness as he deals with my faltering steps here on this earth. When I fail to put on a spirit of gentleness, I look to Jesus. In him alone I find a Savior who is perfect when I am not. In him I find full forgiveness.

We will fail going forth. Daily I fail to put on gentleness (even while writing a Bible study about it!). Yet, each failing is completely forgiven. It is in the peace of this forgiveness that I go forward, in the pursuit of gentleness and the path the Lord wants me to walk, striving to glorify my Lord and Savior to the best of my ability.

Application/ Discussion:

11. Our perfect Savior models gentleness for us. Read John 8:1-11. The Pharisees wanted the woman brought to justice and at the same time showed their contempt for Jesus. How did Jesus put gentleness on display for us here?

12. Reread verse 11. What is your greatest comfort in this verse?

13. What is your favorite verse that describes God's loving pursuit and harrowing rescue of your soul? Write it below. Share with the group and explain why it is meaningful to you.

Gentleness

Key takeaways

- The pursuit of gentleness is a lifelong struggle between acting the way we want and the way God wants us to act.

- Just as God treats us more gently than we deserve, we too put on gentleness in our dealings with the world around us.

- There is great power in gentleness. Look at the quiet waters of baptism and edifying bread and wine of the Lord's supper.

- Jesus pursued us and makes our earthly pursuit of gentleness possible by his grace alone.

- When we fail, Jesus welcomes us back. "I am gentle and humble in heart and you will find rest for your souls" (Matthew 11:29).

Prayer to close   Dear Lord, clothe me with a spirit of gentleness in all I say and do. May my gentle actions leave lasting impressions that lead others to seek you. Forgive me when I falter. Give me the strength and discipline to pursue gentleness every day. In Jesus' name I pray. Amen.

Self-Control

Naomi Schmidt

Definition: *The Spirit-given power to resist temptation*

Prayer to open   Lord Jesus, as we approach this study, tear
down the walls in our hearts and help us admit
our struggle with self-control. We have more
sinful desires than we care to admit—but never
more than are covered by your grace. Deepen
our love for the gospel so that in the face of
temptation we ask, "How could I sin against
God?" Help us live with a joyful desire to obey
you. Burn in our hearts the message that you
are always with us—not just pointing the way
to righteous living but bringing us to grace.
Help us hear your words of truth and remind
us that you are with us and in us, bringing
strength to overcome our sinful desires. In
Jesus' holy name we pray. Amen.

A few stories

With glorious Russian music and stately submarine officers, *The Hunt for Red October* includes a dramatic one-liner delivered with great dignity. Sean Connery says, "Give me a ping, Vasily. One ping only, please." The attention then turns to the sonar officers with massive headphones, focused on that single ping—the sound that will change the direction of the submarine.

Self-Control

Think about that picture as we meditate on God's gift of self-control.

First Corinthians 10:13 says, "God is faithful; he will not let you be tempted beyond what you can bear. But when you are tempted, he will also provide a way out so that you can endure it."

A ping? Will God send a ping when we are about to fall into sin? Nope. No ping will be heard. But listen carefully when you face temptation. Listen for the voice of truth and look for the strong arm of God because when we pray for God's help—whether in a quick moment of temptation or with our daily prayers—we can be confident in his answer. Scripture says, "He *will* provide a way out." Armed with that truth, we know God is with us when we face temptation.

God dwells in our hearts and points to sin—he confronts our sinful thoughts and desires for our spiritual benefit. Through his Spirit he also gives us self-control and enables us to flee temptation. He reminds us: "Sin shall no longer be your master, because you are not under the law, but under grace," and, "Through Christ Jesus the law of the Spirit who gives life has set you free from the law of sin and death" (Romans 6:14; 8:2). Paul encouraged Timothy, "The Spirit God gave us does not make us timid, but gives us power, love and self-discipline" (2 Timothy 1:7).

Throughout history, we see God's powerful work in the lives of believers, giving them self-control and helping them flee temptation.

Throughout history, we see God's powerful work in the lives of believers, giving them self-control and helping them flee temptation. He wrote their accounts to give us hope.

After Joseph's brothers sold him into slavery, he was purchased by Potiphar and put in control of everything Potiphar owned. But Joseph was handsome and well-built, and he caught the eye of his master's wife, who was driven with desire. Day after day she tried to seduce Joseph, but he replied, "With me in charge . . . my master does not concern himself with anything in the house; everything he owns he has entrusted to my care. No one is greater in this house than I am. My master has withheld nothing from me except you, because you are his wife. How then could I do such a wicked thing and sin against God?" (Genesis 39:8,9).

Joseph's desires did not drive his response. His chief concern was for the one he served and the One to whom he belonged. Potiphar trusted Joseph implicitly. How could he possibly sin against him? And even as a slave, Joseph trusted God's plan for his life enough to obey God's commands.

In God's Orchard

Hundreds of years later in this same family line, another beloved son demonstrated self-control rooted in a deep love for God. 1 Samuel chapter 24 tells us that King Saul was trying to kill David. David was running through the hills in Israel, dwelling in caves in an effort to hide from Saul. King Saul went into a cave to relieve himself, unaware that David and his fighting men were hiding in the shadows. In that moment, David could have commanded his men to kill Saul, and he could have taken up the reins over Israel as God's anointed. David's men were eager to assume that the Lord had given Saul into David's hand. But David hesitated, and in an act of self-control, cut a corner from Saul's robe. Even in that action, David was struck with guilt: "The Lord forbid that I should do such a thing to my master, the Lord's anointed" (1 Samuel 24:6). In essence, David followed the prompting of the Spirit and asked, "How could I?"

In the face of temptation too often we ask, "Why not?" instead of, "How could I?" This worldly question spits in the face of consequences and it spits in the face of grace. It says, "Who cares?" to the consequences or to the cost of sin—this is what I want!

We are never far from those sinful urges. Yet Christ calls us his "new creation" (2 Corinthians 5:17). The Holy Spirit gives us the ability to resist sin and transforms our thinking to cherish grace, to hear his "ping," and to ask with our godly forefathers, "How could I?"

Application/Discussion

1. God gave Joseph a dream about his future, and David had been anointed as the next King of Israel. Discuss how our purpose and holy calling shape our thoughts and actions.

2. Maybe your greatest temptation isn't murder or adultery. What do you struggle with, and how does this encouragement from Scripture apply to you?

3. By the power of the Spirit, both men said, *"How could I?"* Our sinful nature says, *"Why not?"* How do we magnify the grace-centered message and silence the sinful one?

The rest of the story

It wasn't many years later when David, our hero of self-control in the cave, fell mightily into temptation with Bathsheba. King David was enjoying the evening air on the palace roof when he noticed Bathsheba bathing nearby and sent for her. His servants brought her to the palace, and David's intentions were clear. Overcome with lust, David listened to his desires and a child was conceived. Then it gets worse.

As is often the case with sin, another sin (in this case, a series of lies and deception) follows close behind. David's sin with Bathsheba ended with the murder of Uriah, who had been a faithful husband and dedicated soldier in David's army. Heartache, shock, and confrontation darken this story, and we see the great King of Israel as an adulterer and murderer.

Overwhelming desire, selfishness, denial, guilt, gut-wrenching sorrow, and disbelief at how far we can fall—have we not all felt these emotions? One moment we are strong, confident in Christ, and filled with spiritual zeal. Then our sinful nature rears its ugly head and fights for control of our hearts and minds. Even strong, Spirit-filled Christians fall. The man who hesitated in the cave now lingers in his lust. The man whose conscience was so clearly in tune with God's will is now dull and dismissive of any prompting by the Holy Spirit. Didn't he hear the booming ping of his servant's words: "She is Bathsheba, the daughter of Eliam and the wife of Uriah" (2 Samuel 11:3)? Where was the voice in his heart calling out, "How could I?"

Whether it happens on the internet, at the office, or behind the secluded curtains drawn around our hearts, we are tempted to daily sin against God. Anger at a coworker, impatience with a child, dishonesty, pride, rage, jealousy—each of us succumbs in our own way. We face a lack of trust in God's faithfulness, unwillingness to believe his Word, or worry over things we cannot control. There is a moment of conflict, sometimes we linger, and then we choose.

In God's Orchard

But the beloved King David is surely not the only example for us. Peter, the passionate fisherman, teaches us too.

Peter, like David, was a godly and respected man. He boldly confessed his faith, "You are the Messiah, the Son of the living God" (Matthew 16:16). He promised he would never leave Jesus, "even if all fall away" (Matthew 26:33). Even in the closing hours of Jesus' life, Peter bloodied his sword to defend Christ in the garden—but all of us know what happened just a few hours later. The rooster crowed and Peter denied his Lord. He called down curses and swore to them, "I don't know this man you're talking about" (Mark 14:71). Where was Peter's "ping"? How could this man who was willing to die by the sword now swear his denial before some servant girl by a fire? Where was the Holy Spirit's gift of self-control now?

And where is the Holy Spirit when you laugh at a dirty joke in the office? Why do you have to express such bitterness when you are irritated with someone you love? We can barely control our words—how can we reign in our thoughts? This is why we have a Savior. We cannot live free of our sinful nature, but we can wholeheartedly cling to the forgiveness and grace of Christ.

Application/Discussion

We cannot live free of our sinful nature, but we can wholeheartedly cling to the forgiveness and grace of Christ.

4. Job declared, "I made a covenant with my eyes not to look lustfully at a young woman" (Job 31:1). What are the pros and cons of creating a covenant like Job's? (You may also marvel that another godly man asks, "How could I?")

5. Discuss Solomon's words of wisdom about self-control:
   a. Proverbs 16:32 says, "Better a patient person than a warrior, one with self-control than one who takes a city." Restate his wisdom using a modern-day comparison.

b. Proverbs 25:28 says, "Like a city whose walls are broken through is a person who lacks self-control." Give a contemporary version of this adage.

6. "Felix was afraid and said, 'That's enough for now! You may leave. When I find it convenient, I will send for you'" (Acts 24:25). Why do you think Felix was afraid and asked Paul to leave? Compare your emotions during a discussion that involves self-control to those of Felix.

The best story

The account of Peter's denial doesn't end in utter sadness. The crowing of the rooster turns the page in the story—and in Peter's heart. Scripture would not have us focus on Peter's guilty conscience but instead turns us to the forgiving look of the Savior as he walks past Peter to the cross (Luke 22:61). Here is our perfect picture of self-control. Here is Jesus, denied by one he deeply loves and still willing to go to the cross to pay for that sin. Could there be a greater example of self-control than Christ, who died for us "while we were still sinners" (Romans 5:8)?

Christ's victory over sin was completed on the cross, but Matthew 4:1-11 also shows us how Jesus had used self-control to beat Satan in the desert. Jesus had fasted for 40 days when Satan challenged him to turn stones into bread, dared him to jump from the pinnacle of a temple, and tried to entice him with worldly wealth. Every word from Jesus' mouth demonstrated perfect self-control and complete reverence for the power of the Word. "*It is written. . . . It is written. . . . It is also written.*" Christ's temptation shows us his perfect self-control which is now ours through faith! We see the Spirit's fruit evident in Christ's life—and we see where to turn in times of temptation as Jesus points to Scripture! And what further comfort do we have as we remember Jesus' temptations? "We do not have a high priest who is unable to empathize with our weaknesses, but we have one who has been tempted in every way, just as we are—yet he did not sin" (Hebrews 4:15). Jesus understands our temptations.

Whether your heart hears a "ping" or a rooster crowing—the Holy Spirit calls us to resist temptation and repent when we fall. Our weakness and shame are washed clean in the living water of grace. Self-control is not a guilt button. It is the gift of the Spirit. He purifies our understanding of this good and powerful gift with his Word. It brings peace and assurance, not the whip of reprimand. We can rejoice in obedient living and freely spend our lives loving Christ and his people. There is no end to the wealth of spiritual gifts God willingly pours into us. And we can turn them toward others.

Application/Discussion

7. How does the thought of Jesus looking at Peter bring you comfort when you realize you have failed to live by the Spirit and not exercised self-control?

> *There is no end to the wealth of spiritual gifts God willingly pours into us.*

8. Like the description of the Holy Spirit's fruit that we are studying, Paul and Peter speak of self-control as part of a big picture that fits together. Read the following passages and discuss how self-control is tied to so many other areas of Christian living.
   a. Titus 2:11,12: Don't miss what "it" is tied to!

   b. 2 Peter 1:5-7: Consider that this is not a vertical or linear list, it's a recipe for a smoothie!

Self-Control

9. Matthew 4:1-11 records three specific temptations Satan spoke to Jesus. Discuss similar temptations that we face. What are other temptations that Jesus faced that you can relate to?

Key takeaways

- God helps us in times of temptation and gives us the ability to resist sin.

- At times we will fall into temptation and choose sin, but God's forgiveness and grace are still ours in Christ.

Prayer to close Lord Jesus, when I hear the term *self-control*, I am drawn to think about the many ways I fail and about the sins I commit. I know I cannot live perfectly, but help me to see self-control as the gift it is. Strengthen my faith through your Word, that I may hear your truth in my heart. Bless me through the Sacraments to trust in your strength and to be confident that you will help in time of need. Though my self-control may be weak in moments of temptation, you have shown yourself to be a powerful and forgiving God. I rest in your care. Thank you for being the Savior I need—and the Savior I love. Amen.

Potential Answers For Love Chapter

1. We need the humility of knowing we are sinners unworthy of God's kindness and gratitude to recognize all God has done for us. If we are self-absorbed, we won't have anything to give to God. We need to realize that service to God matters.

2. Answers will vary, but here's my current list to work on: not being lazy with parenting, putting the best construction on people's words and actions, being more gentle in my communication, and the ongoing work of forgiving completely those who have and continue to hurt me.

3. We can spread the Word, support and encourage those who are in difficult ministry, and be a friend to someone who needs it.

4. Time, advice, mentoring, encouragement—set aside time to spend with the people who need these things. Send a card, an email, or a text. Have coffee with the friend who is going through a hard time.

5. Opening our eyes and noticing needs is first and foremost. Second, we may have to leave our comfort zone. We have to have compassion for someone else in order to want to help them and fill a need.

6. Answers will vary.

7. We have to pursue a passion for the eternal vs. getting caught up in the temporal. It is so easy to be bogged down with worldly worries and discomforts. When we remember the significance of eternal matters, worldly things become less relevant. We should pray for God to help us to see through our stuff so that we see the opportunities he gives us for kingdom work. Then we pray for the strength to do these things when our bodies are weak and tired. "I can do all things through him who gives me strength" (Philippians 4:13).

8. Answers will vary but may include the people who have hurt me, such as an in-law or someone from the church.

Potential Answers for Joy Chapter

1. Answers will vary based on personal experience

2. Answers will vary based on personal experience.

3. Turn to the Word of God. Spend time with it on a daily basis.

4. Remind them what God's Word says about joy and that it is not found in ourselves or the things of this world. Encourage them to spend time connecting to the Word.

5. Answers will vary.

6. Some may respond with answers such as family, material blessings, earthly security, etc. Some people are able to travel a lot.

7. Answers will vary based on personal experience.

8. The only way we can stay connected to the source of our joy is through the Word and Sacraments.

9. Conversations spent discussing the source of joy, then time in the Word. We can also pray for it.

10. Answers may vary. *Shalom* is yours today because of what Jesus has done. You are already reconciled!

Potential Answers for Peace Chapter

1. Jesus had all power but had set aside the use of that power. He was going to take it back again. That Jesus was willing to go from the most powerful to the lowliest position and serve the very sinners he would soon die for is very poignant. How can I not serve others with Jesus as my example?

2. We will be in constant conflict if we don't. We will be like the disciples who argued over who was the greatest. It will take time and energy away from kingdom work. Ultimately, if we are concerned about serving God and not ourselves, submitting is not difficult.

3. When we let God determine what we get, we lose all value in scorekeeping. We will never be content when keeping score. Even if we are getting the short end of the proverbial stick (what, after all, do we deserve?), God is able to repay and give us much more.

4. a. Matthew 6:26,27: Our heavenly Father sees us and will always provide for us. We can trust him to give us what we need when we need it.
   b. Psalm 37:5-6: We need only to follow and walk with God. He will take care of those who take advantage of us.
   c. 1 Peter 5:6: It can be disheartening to feel passed over. If we humbly acknowledge that God is the giver of all things, we will hardly be in the mood to complain. God will put us where we belong at the right time in the right way. We can trust him to do so.

5. When I have exhausted other options, including going to the person to talk about the issues, and I have sought the intervention of others to no avail, sometimes it is in the best interest of all involved to separate. As hard as it is, I should do so with a pure heart, releasing the other person and the situation to God to work out. But put in the work. Don't look at separation as an easy way out.

6. Seek the counsel of a godly friend, pastor, or counselor. Have them help you through the hurt. A godly person will also help you see the other person is not all bad so that you don't villify them. Ask God to

guard your heart. Pray through Psalm 51. A good friend and I have noted that very often the people we have the hardest time with are the ones with a lot of hurt themselves.

7. Pray for the situation and the other person. Seek God in his Word and through prayer. Be open to his chastisement of you and your issues.

8. Answers will vary but may include: not being part of the weekend activities at work. Neighbors thinking you are odd. Being looked down on for Christian values. Your kids being teased about beliefs.

9. Jesus prayed for us. He prayed for us to be strengthened as we seek him. He wanted us to stand and stand apart with the strength he provides.

Potential Answers For Patience Chapter

1. *Webster's Dictionary* defines *long-suffering* as "patiently enduring lasting offense or hardship."[16] The definition of *forbearance* is "the act of forbearing," which means "to control oneself when provoked; be patient."[17] Both terms suitably express the Greek word *makrothumia* in Galatians 5:22. Thinking about these different words for patience can help us better understand all that showing patience in our lives encompasses.

2. Paul endured slander, rejection, multiple imprisonments, severe beatings both by mobs and by the ruling authorities, a stoning attempt, and more. The physical mistreatment brought him near death on more than one occasion. Would Paul have counted these his greatest trials? Or would it have been the imprisonments that curtailed the work of proclaiming Jesus that he so passionately sought to carry out? Paul understood, however, that God was using even persecution of his people to further his kingdom.

3. That person has wronged us, perhaps repeatedly. That person may have wronged people whom we love, such as our child or another family member. Showing patience, however, is an act of will that we choose, not a feeling. Sometimes we must consciously choose over and over to show patient love.

4. Paul never returned evil for evil. He remained focused on his enemies' greatest need—their need for a right relationship with God. He showed his enemies undeserved patience because he was keenly aware of God's undeserved patience toward him. Though he himself had been a persecutor of Christians, God had brought him to faith and given him the privilege of proclaiming Christ. With Paul as our example, we can pray on behalf of those who mistreat us that they come to faith. Sometimes, when someone has mistreated us, we do need to avoid any contact with that person for our own safety and well-being. No matter what the situation, we still can pray for that person's salvation. For ourselves, we can pray that God enables us to understand more fully the undeserved patience that he has shown

[16] https://www.merriam-webster.com/dictionary/long-sufferings.
[17] https://www.merriam-webster.com/dictionary/forbearing

and continues to show us. We can pray that God empty us of anger and bitterness and that he fill us with peace rooted in appreciation of his love.

5. Responses will vary.

6. Instead of complaining or feeling bitter about our thorns, we can consider how it may be drawing us closer to him. It also may be helping us to witness to others, perhaps about Christ's sufficiency in our lives or our hope of heaven where there will be no more pain.

7. Paul did ask for the thorn to be taken away—three times. It is not wrong for us to pray that God remove our thorn, that he cure our chronic illness, that he restore fully our mental health. However, when God's answer is "no," God's promises in Scripture help us accept his answer: in all things, he is working for our good (Romans 8:28); he has a plan for our lives (Jeremiah 29:11); and what he has prepared for us in heaven far outweighs the temporary pain or trouble we must endure now (2 Corinthians 4:16-18). We can take to heart that, while here on earth, God's own power will enable us to bear with patience the pain and difficulty that our thorn brings.

8. In the areas where I am struggling to show patience, I draw not on my own resources, wisdom, and strength but on *God's* power. He freely gives us his own power so that we can bear fruit in every good work (Colossians 1:10), including the fruit of patient endurance.

9. Responses will vary.

10. Jesus prayed for the eternal welfare of the very people who were unjustly putting him to death. As an example to us, we can pray for the salvation of those who have mistreated us, no matter how badly they have hurt us or how heinous their actions.

11. In praying this prayer, Jesus was fulfilling God's law to love even those who hurt us. His fulfillment of God's law in our place throughout his life on earth is called his "active obedience." Jesus prayed this prayer as he was hanging on the cross, accepting God's punishment for all our sins as our substitute. This is called his "passive obedience." Jesus' active and passive obedience were both

Answers

necessary for our salvation; that is, for Jesus' prayer on the cross of "forgive them" to be answered. We are forgiven.

12. We can commit to pray for ourselves and for each other. We can serve as mentors for each other. Most important, however, is that we stay connected to God, our vine (John 15:5). We do this through regular time in his Word and participation in the Lord's Supper. When we make use of these means of grace, we are empowered to bear the fruit of patience in our lives.

Potential Answers for Kindness Chapter

1. Answers will vary.

2. Boaz took notice of Ruth and approached her quickly with practical help. He ensured that she had plenty of food and water while working and plenty of grain at the end of the day by having his men leave extra for her to pick up. He gave her physical protection by telling the men not to touch her. He spoke kindly to her, asking the Lord to bless her. Boaz's faith in a supremely kind God motivated him to show such kindness.

3. At home, we see each other at our "less than best," when we are tired or stressed, making it more challenging to speak and act with kindness. Our family members know how to "push our buttons." And our family members may be less likely than others to show appreciation for our acts of kindness. At these times, we keep in mind that we are not showing them kindness in order to be appreciated but to meet their needs and give glory to God.

4. The people we encounter in our neighborhoods, our schools, and our workplaces are placed there by God. He knows their needs and intends to meet their needs through *us*. He could provide for them himself directly, but he chooses to involve us in his work. This is an amazing, undeserved privilege from our Lord.

5. Answers will vary.

6. Naomi received a new family: Ruth, Boaz, and her grandson, Obed. She had financial and emotional security for the rest of her life and the knowledge that her grandson would carry on the family line and keep the ancestral land in the family. Ruth's status changed from widowed and destitute foreigner to beloved wife and mother of standing in the community. Boaz gained a God-fearing wife and a son.

7. God provides for believers and unbelievers alike, showering all with his gifts. He does so because kindness and faithfulness are innate to his character, *not* because the recipients deserve his kindness. His desire is that these evidences of his love, his "testimony" to the world, will lead all people to acknowledge him as the one true God.

Answers

8. Often, an obstacle we have to showing kindness is our feeling that the recipient—whether a family member or someone at work, school, or church—simply doesn't deserve it. The fact that God shows us kindness that we don't deserve motivates us to do the same for "difficult" people that God has put in our lives. God doesn't "pick and choose" in showing kindness. We pray that he change our attitudes so that we don't "pick and choose" either.

9. God knows our needs much better than we do, and he supplies those needs much better than we can. We turn over our needs to him in prayer and leave them with him. This frees us to focus on meeting the needs of others and being the God-given answer to *their* prayers. A helpful resource on this point is the section entitled, "When is it *my* turn?" (pp. 100-102) from *The Theology of the Cross* by Daniel M. Deutschlander.

10. Boaz had both the willingness and the means to redeem, or buy back, Naomi's husband Ehimelech's ancestral land. Jesus had both the willingness and, as true God, the means to buy us back from sin and death. He redeemed us by his life of perfect obedience to God's law and the shedding of his innocent blood on the cross. Boaz had to be a blood relative of Ehimelech to buy back his land. Jesus is our "blood relative"; he shared our humanity. Boaz chose a foreigner, an outsider of lowly status, to be his bride. Christ chose us, who were by birth outside of God's kingdom and his love. Christ elevated our status to beloved bride and guaranteed our eternal security. These parallels help us better grasp the concept of our redemption and better appreciate the tremendous gifts we have received. For more on these parallels, see *Ruth: Living in God's Unfailing Faithfulness* by Naomi Schmidt (pp. 4, 11).

11. Answers will vary.

12. Passages of God's compassionate love toward us illustrate the kind of love we strive to show others through kind words and actions. Passages of God's eternal commitment to us lead us to renew our commitment to meet the needs of those God has put in our lives. Passages that speak of God's forgiveness comfort us with the knowledge that God sweeps away our sins when we fail to show kindness. Passages that set before us a picture of our home

in heaven encourage us to keep going and remind us that we have only a short while to reflect God's kindness to others here on earth. Always, our motivation for showing kindness is our awed appreciation for God's kindness toward us.

13. The greatest kindness we can show others is to point them to Christ. Performing acts of kindness is one way to "open the door" so that we can share what our kind God has done for us.

Potential Answers for Goodness Chapter

1. Answers will vary.

2. Answers will vary.

3. He promises to always be with us. No matter what we go through, we never go through anything alone. Also, Jesus' death means our eternity is sealed. Even if we—like John the Baptist, Stephen, the apostle Paul, or countless Old Testament prophets—meet a martyr's death, God brings us to be with him for eternity.

4. Answers will vary.

5. Phoebe was a great help. Priscilla and Aquila "risked their lives" for Paul and hosted a congregation in their home. Mary "worked very hard." Andronicus and Junias were in prison with Paul and since they "were in Christ" before Paul, they perhaps encouraged him in his early faith. Tryphena, Tryphosa, and Persis also worked very hard in the Lord. Rufus' mother was like a mother to Paul. Answers will vary but may include coming alongside and supporting those in ministry. Encourage, support, and befriend called workers.

6. We can do nothing on our own, but through God's goodness in Christ and the working of the Holy Spirit in Word and sacrament, we can daily drown our old Adam and live a new life.

7. The greatest good work we can do is to tell others about Christ. Sometimes I do it well, but if I'm honest, there's room for improvement. My every conversation should point the world to Jesus. Lord, help me!

8. God has already equipped us to do his work. Our excuses are just that—excuses. If we look at God's conversation with Moses from the burning bush (Exodus 3), we see God is not impressed with our excuses. He gave us what we need to do his work, and he expects us to do so.

9. Talk about ways in which you can help others. Often, when I hear what someone else has done, it encourages me to act too. Give each other ideas. Tell others about the things that have been

encouraging to you. And remind each other of what Jesus has done for us, directly and indirectly through others.

Answers

Potential Answers for Faithfulness Chapter

1. Today, there may be a marriage that doesn't meet our needs or makes us miserable. An affair springs up and a lonely heart turns from the Lord to desperately grasp for tangible love. Financial trouble may drive people to dishonesty. People who unwilling to tell the truth get caught up in a vicious cycle of lies and deceit. Pride and hardened hearts keep people from confessing their sin and finding peace in forgiveness—they would rather try to make it up somehow, justify themselves, or declare themselves righteous. Help participants understand that even when they fail, God will be faithful to them.

2. Read the following passages about God's unfailing faithfulness:
   a. Deuteronomy 32:4: God is strong and dependable. Everything he does is right; he doesn't make mistakes. When things are going in a direction that doesn't seem right, we can trust God because we know he is faithful, not because we understand what he is doing.

   b. Psalm 89:8: God's power is boundless, and he understands things we cannot comprehend. Because he is both mighty and faithful, he is able to do what he knows is best, though we are unable to help ourselves or unsure of what to do.

   c. 1 Corinthians 1:8,9: God won't leave us at any point in our faith journey. He will faithfully carry us to the very end because of what Jesus has done.

   d. 1 Corinthians 10:13: God is beside us when we are tempted. He helps us to do the right thing and reminds us that we can chose not to sin. He gives us his power when we face temptation and faithfully helps us to stand strong. He will not let Satan snatch us from his hand but teaches us about his strength and faithfulness in our hardship.

   e. 1 John 1:9: All is forgiven: every sin we ever commit God wipes away because of Jesus. He is always faithful to forgive.

3. He longs to be gracious to you; he will rise up to show you compassion; blessed are all who wait for him; you will weep no more; as soon as he hears, he will answer you.

In God's Orchard

4. We are saint and sinner. Never lose sight of the fact that we are *both!* But as believers, we cling to the forgiveness and righteousness given to us by Christ—we are repentant Gomers; we are restored to faithfulness like Hosea! When we fail, God forgives us. Don't let Satan keep you in the bondage of guilt and self-condemnation if you are a Gomer. You are forgiven and free. And if you are a Hosea, don't fall into the trap of the older brother in Jesus' parable of the prodigal son. We are not in any way better than the Gomers. Our righteousness is based on Jesus and Jesus alone.

5. Answers will vary.

6. Motivated by grace, we will do what is right and honorable. We will follow through when we have promised to do something, stand by our friends in hardship, and remind them of grace when they fall. We will put the needs of others first and live in a way that reflects God's faithfulness and points people to Christ.

7. Answers will vary but could include loving others, time management, employment issues, political resentment, or stewardship of gifts. It might also be a lack of faithfulness regarding God's Word, compassion, or having a poor attitude. Be sure to close the discussion with the reminder that *all* our unfaithfulness has been paid for by Christ. None of our failures are outside the realm of his forgiveness.

8. Every moment can be filled with thoughts of God's faithfulness and a desire to live by the power of his Spirit. It is dependability, commitment, and godly priorities. But even more—it is a characteristic that reflects the nature of God.

Answers

Potential Answers for Gentleness Chapter

1. Answers will vary.

2. Answers will vary.

3. A harsh word stirs up anger. Gentleness breeds peace and harmony in our earthly relationships as it turns away wrath.

4. The love of money can cause us to fall into temptation, plunge us into ruin and destruction, cause us to wander from the faith, and pierce us with many griefs.

5. Righteousness, godliness, faith, love, endurance, and gentleness. These come through the working of the Holy Spirit. We pursue these by increasing our diet of God's Word through devotions; public worship; Bible study in church, in private, and with our friends; and by receiving the Sacrament regularly.

6. Paul tells us that this pursuit will be a fight. Our walk of faith is a daily fight against sin, death, and the devil. We will fight these battles daily, but God has already won the victory for us on the cross.

7. Answers will vary but may include that God harnessed his power and spoke gently to his broken prophet. Also, he pointed out that Elijah only knew part of the truth. Elijah saw Jezebel and felt alone. God told him there were others who were faithful and not worshiping idols.

8. Answers will vary.

9. Answers will vary.

10. Answers will vary but may include sending someone to confront us and bring us back to him. He speaks to us through the Word. Sometimes he points us to a sermon, blog, podcast, or another Christian to guide us.

11. Jesus showed his great love for sinners here. He shows wisdom as he answered the Pharisees who wanted to trap him. He showed love for this sinful woman as he reminded her that her sins were forgiven.

12. Notice that Jesus didn't fail to deal with the woman's sin. He declared her forgiveness but encouraged her to leave the life of sin. This is a beautiful picture of gentleness. Jesus acted softly out of love for the woman's soul.

13. Answers will vary.

Answers

Potential Answers for Self-Control Chapter

1. Our purpose and calling in Christ is just as certain and holy as the calls God gave to Joseph and David. We are called to be a holy nation that proclaims the light of Christ. We are salt in a world that is decaying before our eyes. With such a holy and important calling, given to us at such a great cost, how could we sin against God?

2. Sin is sin. James 2:10 tells us, "Whoever keeps the whole law and yet stumbles at just one point is guilty of breaking all of it." We all need to be reminded of our need for a Savior and see that all temptations are threatening because willful sin eats away at faith. These accounts remind us that God is with us in whatever moments of temptations that arise. Each of us will find temptations that are more difficult for us. We must always be on guard. But when we focus on God and what he has done for us, he will be with us to help us avoid temptation.

3. We feed on the Word of God and bathe our hearts with the forgiveness of Christ. We can also choose to surround ourselves with people and environments that keep us focused on Christ. As we are in the world, being a light in darkness, we will remember God is with us and be aware of temptations.

4. Find the healthy balance between human practices meant to help us and the danger of becoming focused on our efforts and strength, concerned more with our obedience than God's gift of grace. Everything is permissible; not everything is beneficial" (1 Corinthians 10:23). Making a promise to God may be helpful, but don't create laws where there are none.

5. Proverbs 16:32: "Better a patient person than a warrior, one with self-control than one who takes a city."
   Have participants complete the sentence, "Better a person with self-control than _____ " (wealth, power, influence, intelligence, abilities, etc.). Think of things in this life that have less value when there is no self-control. Consider the example of business executives, politicians, pastors, athletes, or celebrities whose lives are destroyed because of their personal lives.

In God's Orchard

Proverbs 25:28: "Like a city whose walls are broken through is a person who lacks self-control." The image is like someone who leaves their back door unlocked even when the rest of the house is secure, or they have a home security system but don't turn it on. They are vulnerable, defenseless, and at risk. You can also discuss how someone might look at the rest of the city wall (other areas of life where they are secure) and think they are safe because they deny the hole in the wall. They have wealth or prestige, but the "hole in the city wall" is drug use, embezzlement, or an affair (or any ongoing willful sin!) that will destroy them.

6. The conversation was getting uncomfortable because it involved the discussion of righteousness and judgment. Felix's conscience was starting to bother him. Our study of self-control gives us confidence because it points to the powerful help of God, not our flailing efforts to be self-controlled. We don't have to be afraid to talk about judgment and holy living because our confidence is in Christ! Remember when you talk to others about Christ, openly admit your need for a Savior.

7. It pierces our hearts with the purity and depth of Christ's love for us when we are so undeserving. It is an image of the complete and holy forgiveness of Christ in the moment of our sin, knowing that he will have to bear the full weight and punishment of our guilt. But his love reigns! He loved Peter perfectly and forgave him completely— just like he loves and forgives us perfectly!

8. Titus 2:11,12: "The grace of God has appeared that offers salvation to all people. It teaches us to say "no" to ungodliness and worldly passions, and to live self-controlled, upright and godly lives in this present age." Self-control is tied to grace—it is a gift, not a demand! The gift of salvation motivates us to say no to ungodliness, it teaches us to resist worldly passions and live God-pleasing lives "in this present age."

2 Peter 1:5-7: "For this very reason, make every effort to add to your faith goodness; and to goodness, knowledge; and to knowledge, self-control; and to self-control, perseverance; and to perseverance, godliness; and to godliness, mutual affection; and to mutual affection, love."

Answers

This is not a task-by-task list of instructions. Love is certainly not the last thing that is added to our faith. But as all these aspects of Christian living come together under the gift of grace, God is honored and our lives will draw attention to him (this is what it means to "glorify God" in our lives). There are great blessings in Christian living.

9. We are tempted to worry about our physical/financial needs, or perhaps we are facing illness and need healing. Does Satan tempt us to covet earthly wealth? We can "test" God in our attitudes and actions when we openly sin and expect grace, when we mistreat our bodies and expect to be healthy, or when we spend lavishly and expect him to provide. We can relate to the struggle of being overworked, overtired, and hungry—all these bring temptations! Answers will vary.